THE
MAGIC OF
ANGELS

THE MAGIC OF ANGELS

How to recognise and harness
your own angelic powers

Adele Nozedar

metro

Published by Metro Publishing
an imprint of John Blake Publishing Ltd
3 Bramber Court, 2 Bramber Road,
London W14 9PB, England

www.johnblakepublishing.co.uk

First published in paperback in 2010

ISBN 978 1 84454 899 6

British Library Cataloguing-in-Publication Data:
A catalogue record for this book is available from the British Library.

Design by www.envydesign.co.uk

Printed in Great Britain by CPI Bookmarque, Croydon CR0 4TD

1 3 5 7 9 10 8 6 4 2

Papers used by John Blake Publishing are natural, recyclable products
made from wood grown in sustainable forests. The manufacturing processes
conform to the environmental regulations of the country of origin.

Every attempt has been made to contact the relevant copyright-holders,
but some were unobtainable. We would be grateful if the
appropriate people could contact us.

For Theo Chalmers, Lisa Johnson
and Jon Whittington

CONTENTS

PART TWO

ACCESSING AND HARNESSING YOUR OWN ANGELIC POWERS

Disclaimer

There is very little that is objective about this book. Much of it is born from personal experience, and deals with matters that cannot be satisfactorily explained, or weighed, or measured, or set against anything else, or put in a box. We have lived with angels – and demons – for thousands of years, and yet there are still no rules.

The content of this book has been driven purely by what I found out during the course of my research. I don't apologise for this, but felt it important to tell you that this is no scientific or empirical study. Also, I am no metaphysician, but I do know from my own experience that there are even more extraordinary wonders in this universe than the ones that we can detect with our human senses alone.

The stories in these pages will make you laugh, cry, wonder...and this book might just change your life.

Foreword

Spirits in the Sky

'The best advice to sceptics and curious folk is to look within, find your basic instincts and to trust them when they tell you that something you may not have believed before is true. Expect a revelation!

We have to be vigilant, to keep our senses, mind and heart open.

Don't be scared to speak out. Organised religions, along with the establishments based upon them, have spent thousands of years suppressing our natural instincts and establishing a 'norm' that tries to banish credibility in anything other than what they want us to believe. They have been forced to incorporate Angels into their teachings and shape them into servants of their regimes, since the evidence for their existence is absolutely over-whelming and they would have lost credibility had they not done so.

May this magical book free the Angels from their bondage of religious dogma.'

The Reverend Doctor Clive Thomas Jackson,
'Dr and the Medics'

Introduction

The Realms of Angels: where nothing is ever black or white

'I think it was Heraclitus who said: the Daimon is our destiny.
When I think of life as a struggle with the Daimon who would ever
set us to the hardest work among those not impossible, I understand
why there is a deep enmity between a man and his destiny, and
why a man loves nothing but his destiny... I am persuaded that
the Daimon delivers and deceives us, and that he wove the netting
from the stars and threw the net from his shoulder...'
—W. B. YEATS, *Mythologies*, 1959

I thought that I had had sufficient experiences of my own involving angelic energies to be able to speak with some authority on the subject, and to pinpoint the right stories to use when researching the many anecdotes that came my way whilst researching this book. You can tell when something rings true.

Nevertheless, when I began putting this book together I was given a warning by someone with far more experience in these matters. I was told that, once I started to investigate the angelic realms very seriously, once I started to consciously 'offer myself up' to their influences, then things would start to change and shift. I was told that these changes and shifts were necessary evidence of Angels manifesting their presence in my life. The journey which had brought me to the position of being able to write this book was also a part of a greater influence, and all moments converge to create the moment that we're living in.

I took this advice seriously purely because of the credibility of the person that gave it to me, and so I made a conscious effort to open the doors of my own perception. Dramatic events ensued, so much so that the final lines of this book were written from a hospital bed!

Hospitals are charged, edgy places. All human endeavour is focused in a place like this. Life and death; overwhelming joy and deep pain; huge happiness, overwhelming sadness, the struggle to come to terms with mortality. In the nights I have spent here unable to sleep I have travelled in my mind to the places where my body couldn't take me, floated through the hospital corridors with its ghosts of the living, the dead and the dying, and actually had the encounters with the angels that I had asked for, and with the very welcome demons that came along as well.

I can see now that the proximity of these angels was what made the demons draw closer, too. Demons that I had suppressed for pretty much all of my life came to the fore, and catalysed more changes. And yet what's interesting for me to observe is that the angels in my life now seem to be working in symbiosis with those demons in order to effect some kind of integration, and this process is not happening in isolation. Every single person in the entire world is involved, especially you, reading this. It's a shock sometimes to realise that any process that you or I choose to undergo is never about the individual, but about everyone, even though one individual might have triggered it by asking for something, some experience, some evidence of something extraordinary. It's true that one person can change the world.

Be careful what you ask for, because angels can be stern masters. They will challenge you, play pig-in-the-middle with your ego, relentlessly hack away at your preconceived ideas, ask you to think, and think again, and then stop thinking altogether; they will briskly strip your psyche apart like so many bits of an engine, and, if you allow them to and can bear the pain, they will rebuild you, better, bigger and brighter than before.

We tend to turn to angels for guidance during the dark times of our lives. Maybe this is why you are holding this book. It's as well to remember, though, that throughout all the darkness, it's vital to realise we need to have faith not only in the future, but in the present, that everything is as it is meant to be and that hard times are only difficult if we choose to see them as such. And those demons, if we try to suppress or bury them, get angry and pursue us – sometimes even down the generations.

If we are to work with angels – and I will put forward here and now the idea that they are working with us, all the time, whether we acknowledge it or not – then it is essential that we embrace those demons, too, since they are just as important.

Throughout this book, I will ask you to think again about the way in which we perceive demons. It's no accident that in ancient literatures, demons and angels are often mistaken for one another, and often share names and attributes. It's no accident, either, that all the skills that we attribute to 'witchcraft' or the 'dark arts' – such as healing, prophecy, prediction – were legendarily taught to humankind (specifically to women) by certain angels.

A Profound Difference

What separates human beings from other animals is that we have freedom of choice. Although we have pheromones and emotional charges and powerful reactions, we do not need to eat as much as can find as soon as we find it, or mate in the street haphazardly like dogs with bitches on heat. If ever anyone tells you that they 'didn't have a choice', then beware, for you're hearing a lie. When we say we have no choice, it's an absolution of responsibility and a denial of our own power. We always have choice.

As we've seen, we can choose also how we view things and therefore alter our experience of them. Demons can be the things that make 'bad' things happen; it's within our gift to make these things good.

Thought forms are very powerful. Later on in this book is the description of a demonic thought form that was created entirely by human beings. These evil thought forms can become real enough, and their influence, if not recognised, can cast a long shadow down the generations. Child abuse is a good example. How can it be possible to find the 'gift' within such a horrendous act or experience?

Until we are strong enough and courageous enough to take these man-made demons, face them, give them a name, turn them upside down and rattle their cages and shake and shake and shake them until their teeth ache, they will rule us. But once we do all these things then we will discover the core of goodness inside something which had appeared to be rotten through and through.

This can be extraordinarily difficult and we cannot deny the existence of the horrors that we are responsible for, since to do so would be a lie. Take the Nazi Holocaust, for example. The evil that was in Hitler's mind wasn't spread by supernatural forces, and it's dangerously stupid to suggest that it was – because once again it's like saying 'there was no choice'. If we say this, we absolve ourselves of responsibility, blaming outside forces 'bigger than us', and we ignore the horrendous chain of events that can happen when, as human beings with freedom of choice, we choose to be lead by charismatic ideas, flattery, and promises of a better future. When we are weak and easily led rather than being strong and aware enough to stand up to the forces of evil which are far worse in mankind than any supernatural force – or 'demon' – could account for.

We need to learn to make judgments from our own innate, internal set of scales, between what's right and what isn't. Remove the ego or the attachment to conditions, and the pearl of truth is the thing that's left. If we regard any outside influence as an arbiter of truth, then this can be faulty and subject to misinterpretation. Frighteningly, Stanley Milgram's experiments in the early 1960s showed that many people would follow the orders of an authority figure even if these orders violated their profoundest moral beliefs. Milgram was able to get one group of people to potentially administer a lethal electric shock to another group by the simple method of having an official-looking man in a white coat issue the order. Sinister. We need to be vigilant, question everything. But the dilemma here, as my friend Simon points out, is that Milgram's experiment effectively sets out to prove that we *don't* really have choices. Is this true? I'm not sure. Maybe the only thing we can do is test everything; listen to the voice of truth that's inside every single one of us.

When we hear tell of that 'still small voice', it's a reference to the spark of the divine which is inside of all of us, and which holds the truth. In this mirror of truth, both angels and demons are reflected. If we look beyond our material, black and white, earthly world, the world where we like to categorise everything and put it into a box, we will see that both angels and demons are very closely aligned. As patterns are defined by the shadows they make as light is shone, the angel and the demon cannot exist without one another. We need have no fear of either but, again, hold onto faith in the present, trust our intuition and judgment, and let the future sort itself out.

'We Are All Made Of Stars'
——MOBY, from the song of the same name

You will notice that there's a list of names running along the bottom of the pages of this book. These names are those people who, during their lifetimes, have shown evidence of angelic energies, powers outside of the 'normal' remit of what's accepted as standard human experience. Some of these people are famous. Some of them are not. The names were suggested not by me, but by a wide-ranging group of people from all around the world. Some of the names – such as that of the Dalai Lama – appeared over and over again. Some of them, of course, appeared only once. But all these people are a reminder that angelic powers are part of our birthright, essential to our very existence. I hope that this book will help you to recognise and realise the part of *you* that is bigger, brighter, better, outside of the usual everyday petty concerns, the part of you that looks beyond all this and which constantly scans the horizon for the bigger picture.

I hope this book will help you tap into the angelic energy that's inside you.

There are many people whom I need to thank. Firstly, the inestimable Special Agent Isabel Atherton at Creative Authors, and all the crew at John Blake.

There are hundreds, if not thousands, of amazing angel books on the market. Because I wanted to do something very different with this one, I was looking for anecdotes that were edgier, spikier, sharper than ones I'd seen elsewhere. I feel very privileged to have had the confidence of some absolutely extraordinary people, most of them complete strangers, and I hope that you will understand the reasons why some of these contributors have chosen to remain anonymous. I owe a huge debt of thanks to the many people that responded to my requests for stories, whether or not I was able to use them here. To all those unnamed people whose stories feature in this book – I thank you for the trust that you placed in me.

There are other contributors, too, many of whom are actually named in the text. I would especially like to mention Beverli Rhodes, who courageously shared her harrowing experience of being trapped in the London bombings of 2007, and also Lynne Lauren, whose advice about meditation provided a huge amount of inspiration for me on many different levels. Her own book, *Simply Meditation*, is absolutely essential reading. Rhiannon Davies showed profound generosity in sharing her traumatic but inspiring story, and I thank her from the bottom of my heart. I'd also like to thank Tania Ahsan at *Kindred Spirit*, and to the readers of the magazine who sent me their stories. I also need to thank *Rolling Stone* magazine for the information about Carlos Santana, and the *Daily Mail* newspaper for the information about Noel Edmonds.

Theo Chalmers of Verve PR's guidance and wise words have been invaluable; yet again, a huge debt of thanks. Speaking of angelic influences, the new Muse album was released at just the right time to inspire the final wrestle with this book; thanks guys. The very last little bits of this book were written whilst I was in hospital, so I'd like to thank the incredibly angelic nurses, doctors and all the support staff at the Nevill Hall Hospital, Abergavenny. These people are truly the agents of celestial forces.

Sometimes the machinations of those angels are quite mystifying. And so I need to say thanks to the baffling persistence of Simon Clayton, his remarkable daughter Esti, and her magical ferrets.

Finally, I would like to express my undying love and gratitude to the man to whom this book is dedicated, my amazing husband, Adam Fuest. May the adventure continue!

Adele Nozedar
26th December 2009

PART ONE
INVESTIGATING ANGELS

*'It is hereby decreed that the wall separating
the sacred and the profane be torn down.
From now on, everything will be sacred.'*
—PAULO COELHO

1
Angelic Energy
A Personal Experience

As a writer and researcher with a strong interest in the paranormal, I approach my investigations into angels with the same attitude that I apply to such matters as ghosts, spirits, evidence of witchcraft, or the meanings of arcane symbols. The reason for my interest in these fascinating subjects is very much based on my own experiences. Sometimes I am lucky (or unlucky) enough to be able to see and feel certain things that some people can't, or to look at things in a different way, and I'm driven by an insatiable curiosity to understand the unseen world that surrounds us.

I like to think that I have a mind that is open enough to encompass any possibility, but with an effective credibility filter that enables me to reject anything that is obviously nonsense. My experience tells me that there are some things which exist outside of the parameters of our everyday experience, and which can't be fully explained despite all the scientific and rational tools we have amassed. So, sometimes, we set up a framework whereby we are able to explain things. After all, if

Zoroaster • *John Dee* • *Nancy Palmer-Jones* • *Adam Fuest*

we can find a way to rationalise something, we think we can exert some sort of control over it.

We all think in different ways; one person's incident of angelic intervention, for example, might be mere coincidence to another. And I've also realised that we can choose how we interpret absolutely anything at all in this world of ours.

Some time ago, I placed an ad in a popular magazine that deals in stories of the paranormal and of extraordinary events. In the ad, I asked for stories of angels, and got a significant response.

There was a catalyst for my interest in angels and the way that they manifest. I'd like to tell you this short story, and you're welcome to analyse it however you like. The reason I've chosen it is because it pulls together many of the elements that really do speak of angelic energies at work; karma, coincidences, help arriving unexpectedly when you most need it and least expect it – and the seeming intervention of a Hindu god. In addition, it seems only fair that if I'm asking for other people's stories, I include some of my own.

I have marked the series of incidents which serve to lift this particular story out of the ordinary and into the realms of the extraordinary. I'm not going to call the incidents 'miracles'. I'll leave that for you to decide. I have changed the names of those involved in the story.

I'll also leave it for you to decide whether these true events contain elements of angelic intervention, or sheer coincidence. *You might even decide that they are the same thing.*

In 2003, I was due to go to India for a month to study yoga. I happened to mention this to Sarah, a wonderful woman I knew who was quite a bit older than me, then aged about 65. She had visited India after the death of her husband five or so years before. Sarah had been determined not to mope, viewing the death

Jeanne McKenzie • Robert Atherton • Doreen Virtue • Jacqui Newcombe

instead as a reminder of her own mortality, a reason to squeeze the value out of every minute she had left. Sarah went into training, hauling rucksacks full of rocks up and down the mountains of South Wales so that she could get fit for her three-month trip backpacking around south India. She was a complete inspiration.

When I mentioned that I was going to India, Sarah told me immediately that she was going to come with me. I was surprised, but delighted to have such a lovely travelling companion.

All went well. India is a magical place where, it seems, anything can happen. I did lots of yoga, toured temples and holy places, and saw a conjunction of Mars and Venus in a clear dark sky. Sarah joined in the yoga too, had a nostalgic time visiting old haunts and friends that she'd last seen five years before, and we joined up again towards the end of the trip.

A day or so before we were due to return to the UK, we were staying in a small, two-storey grass-roofed bamboo hut on the edge of the beach just south of Pondicherry. The manageress of the place lived on the ground floor. We accessed our little eyrie, about four metres from the ground, using a rickety bamboo ladder. Sea eagles regularly flew around our temporary home.

One afternoon, as Sarah started to climb down, the ladder snapped. There was a wrenching sound as the bamboo broke, and a dull, sickening thump, and there lay my friend, motionless. She had been deposited, head first, onto the concrete ground below. A pool of blood was spreading around Sarah's head. I thought she was dead.

This was the first time in my life that I had been faced with a real disaster, and I was pleased to remember, afterwards, that I was completely calm, with an instinctive knowledge of what I needed to do. I checked Sarah's pulse, found a shade to keep her out of the burning sun, and then ran into the home of the manageress of the place, a Russian woman. I ran straight past her

Diana Cooper • *The Prophet* • *Roald Dahl* • *Paulo Coelho*

and hauled a bag of ice from her freezer to apply to Sarah's head.

The woman, Nadia, ran outside after me, shouting, 'What are you doing?' Then she saw the motionless body and the pool of blood which had spread widely and dangerously, and she immediately started screaming.

I didn't hesitate. I grabbed Nadia by the shoulder and slapped her hard across the face. If Sarah was conscious, the screaming would frighten her. If she wasn't conscious, then no amount of screaming was going to help. Actually, I really enjoyed that slap.

By now a few of the local fishermen and their wives had gathered, accompanied by the ubiquitous crowd of kids that converge at a moment's notice anywhere in India. I commandeered a motorbike to take me the half mile or so back to the ashram where I'd been staying, and where one of the main teachers was also a medical doctor.

When I arrived at the Ashram, there were three people standing outside. I had forgotten that it was a major Ganesha festival, akin to Christmas Eve; consequently, everyone had left the building and the three remaining people were waiting for a taxi to take them to the party. One of the ladies, Melanie, took me inside and seemed to be taking an age to try to call anyone who could help; there was no reply from any of the hospitals.

'If Sarah dies, she will die in a good place. Everyone has to die sometime'. Melanie's words made me very angry. I grabbed the phone and the phone book and found a home number for Ananda, the teacher who was also a doctor. Despite the emergency, Melanie had told me not to call him as he'd be unavailable because of the festivities.

Incident Number One

Ananda picked up straight away. Later, it transpired that he had been on his way to the festivities when 'something' told him he

Jesus Christ • *Jeremy Clarkson* • *Patti Smith* • *Tim Smit*

should go back home. Although he'd laughed at himself for being fanciful, nevertheless he obeyed his instincts and heard the phone start ringing as soon as he got through the door.

Because of his work with a local hospital, Ananda could get straight through to a department that promised to send an ambulance. In the meantime, I jumped on the motorbike and raced back to Sarah, who was barely conscious; I peeled back an eyelid and she looked glazed. She couldn't talk, although her nursing training had given her the presence of mind to ask that she be shaded by an umbrella. Soon Ananda arrived with the small, van-like ambulance in tow. Sarah's head was bandaged in a plastic bin bag because there was so much blood that cloth alone wasn't good enough. And she was taken to the hospital.

Here is not the place to describe the full horror of a rural Indian hospital. But it wasn't nice. There was blood – and other substances – on the walls and floor. People lay in the corridors, without blankets or mattresses, waiting for attention. Unless patients had a companion to help them in the hospital, there was no treatment. Accordingly, I saw Sarah set up in the life support department – although the equipment, compared to Western standards, looked frighteningly inadequate.

By now it was dark, and I sat down on the hard floor outside Sarah's room. All I could do was wait. I couldn't make any calls; I didn't have a mobile with me, and the only place to make calls was a half a mile or so from the hospital. And it was closed. In any case, I didn't really want to have to call Sarah's family to tell them she was on a primitive life support machine in a filthy foreign hospital. What would they be able to do except panic? I told myself, optimistically, that I'd call them when she was in a better state.

Suddenly, the door to Sarah's room was flung open and a doctor came out. He thrust a piece of paper into my hand. 'Hurry – you need to buy this from the dispensary. It's urgent.'

Anita   Roddick   •   Alexandra   David-Neal   •   Dalai   Lama

Without waiting to tell me where the dispensary was, the doctor whisked back into the room. Just before he closed the door I could see people rushing around a prone figure on a stretcher. I ran like hell and pounded at the door of the little wooden shop at the edge of the hospital grounds. The pharmacist, who had obviously been asleep on the floor, rubbed his eyes, read the paper, and disappeared into a back room. After what seemed like an age, he reappeared.

Incident Number Two

'We don't have this drug; I just ran out. I'm sorry. It's the only thing I don't have here'.

Now I panicked. What chance did Sarah have if they had run out of the drug she needed?

'Can you look again? This is life or death…Have you got an alternative?'

The pharmacist didn't seem to have the same sense of urgency as me. Grumbling a little, he disappeared again, returning with a small package.

'This isn't as effective, but tell the doctor it will do for now'.

Then he disappeared back inside and slammed the shutters in front of me. Breathless after running, I thrust the package into the doctor's hand, which looked at it and shook his head. 'This might be OK; it might not. Pray for your friend; she is sliding into a coma'.

There was no way I was going to sleep that night. I wandered out into the cool, fragrant Indian air, and sat under a tree by the light of the full moon. I am not the praying type, but I did say a prayer to whatever Gods might be listening.

I suddenly realised I'd need to try to contact Sarah's insurance company. I had grabbed some of her bags when we'd rushed to the hospital and now it was necessary to find the paperwork, so

Barack Obama • *Jules Verne* • *Frances Drake* • *Dylan Thomas*

I started to see if I could find anything. I rooted through clothes, books, toiletries. Tucked at the bottom of the bag was an old large-sized Flora margarine tub with an elastic band round it; on the top was a label that read 'Documents'. Inside was Sarah's passport, her flight tickets, her insurance documents....and a list of the medications that she was taking for a heart condition.

This was something I hadn't known about. Sarah had never told me. I saw she was on warfarin, a drug that thins the blood and stops it from clotting. Maybe this would explain the vast quantity of blood that had poured like water from her wound. Maybe the doctor would need to know about this.

Tucked inside Sarah's passport was another slip of paper. On it was a list of drugs that she was allergic to.

Incident Number Three

At the top of the list was a familiar name. I took out the crumpled prescription from my pocket. The drug that had been unavailable could possibly have killed Sarah outright.

A couple of days later, Sarah's condition seemed to have stabilised. She was out of life support and lay on a pallet bed on the floor of a room full of other people; I had to pick my way over sleeping people to get to her. Things were getting very difficult for me. I was determined to read the slip for every drug that entered her body. I was also responsible for washing my friend, difficult in a place where one cold stand pipe served at least 50 people. She was unable to feed herself, or even take a sip of water. I had to make trips to the pharmacy four or five times a day, and had to call the insurance company and Sarah's family from the small phone centre, which had a continual queue.

My own situation was far from comfortable. I was unable to sleep, unable to wash, eating very little since I had hardly any money left to spend at the canteen; medication had to take

Robbie Burns • *T.S. Eliot* • *Jeremy Sandford* • *Bruce Chatwin*

priority. I was surrounded by terribly sick people. Added to this, the nine-hour time difference between India and the UK was making communication difficult. The insurance company, snug in their offices in England, had no idea of the conditions in an Indian hospital. They were worse than useless.

I hated to leave Sarah alone while I tried to juggle everything, but had no option. After I had spent a couple of hours trying, and once again failing, to get through to the insurance company, I remember thinking, divine intervention could be a really handy thing right now.

At the top of the steps to the hospital was a statue of Ganesh, the elephant-headed God who is believed to remove obstacles.

'Come on, Ganesh, you bastard; give me a break. Get me a mobile phone from somewhere, will you, and a bundle of cash?' I didn't believe for a minute in Ganesh, and I am not superstitious; I said it as a release of anger after the frustration and tension of the past few days.

When I got back to Sarah, a girl was sitting by her. The girl was wearing a blue sari and had a long black plait. I assumed that she was Indian. But then she spoke, and she had an accent somewhere between French and German.

'Hi', she said. 'I'm Eva. I heard about what happened at the huts, and I thought I'd see if I could help. I've been in Indian hospitals before, and know how difficult it can be. Is there anything I can do?'

The very presence of Eva seemed at that moment to be a miracle; the prospect of someone who might be able to keep an eye on Sarah whilst I attempted to contact the insurance company and negotiated with the hospital to put her in a decent room, was such a relief.

'Yes — you can help!'

I asked Eva to help with watching over Sarah, and gave her a

Beryl Nozedar • *Trevor Nozedar* • *Andrew Catlin* • *Edith Piaf*

list of the drugs that she was allergic to. I asked her to make sure that Sarah got water to her lips, since she was still far too weak to help herself. As an afterthought, I asked if she might have a spare mobile phone.

Incident Number Four

Without a word, Eva handed me her phone. 'I topped it up this morning so there's plenty of time on it. Oh, and why don't you let me lend you some cash? I've plenty. You can pay me back another time'.

Within minutes of my angry throwaway plea to a stone statue, I'd been given the three things I asked for: help, a phone, and money.

Talking to Eva later, I found that she was Swiss, from Lucerne. She worked in a cinema called Twin Peaks; we own a recording studio called Twin Peaks.

Eva came to the hospital every day. It was just as well, because Sarah wasn't off the critical list yet. She was back on life support for a while before being transferred to a better room, since thanks to Eva I'd been able to speak to the superintendant of the hospital (after waiting outside his door for a full day).

After I'd spent three weeks in the hospital, sleeping under a tree, Sarah's daughter flew out from the UK and I was able to return home. Eventually, Sarah recovered, but not before she'd had brain surgery and a blood transfusion. In fact, the new haircut that she had after they had to shave her head took years off her!

Incident Number Five – And Six

A couple of end notes. Retrospectively, I discovered some pieces of the back story to some of these happenings. The reason that the Russian manageress of the huts had become so hysterical? A few days before the ladder broke, she had had a dream in which a lady

Billie Holiday • *James Watt* • *Louis Armstrong* • *The Searys*

lay in a pool of blood. She had actually known that the ladder was faulty, but ignored the message in her dream. When the accident happened in real life, she couldn't work out if it was real, or if it was the nightmare come back again. Maybe it was both.

Eva, who really did turn up like an angel and to whom I believe Sarah owes her life, gave me her email address. I mailed several times from the UK, but the message always bounced back.

So I thought to call her at the Twin Peaks Cinema in Lucerne. There is no such place.

Was Eva an actual angel? I can't answer that. Did she manifest angelic energy, and was I able to harness it for my own needs? That's a definite 'Yes'.

The following stories in this book will inspire you, and provoke you to think again, to see the world in a different light. And you will discover how to find your own angels, and how to harness that angelic energy for yourself.

Theo Chalmers • Janet Gleghorn • Edmund Hilary

2

What *is* an Angel?

G ood question, and one that we'll be spending the rest of this book trying to answer. But for now, let's keep it simple and try to think of a few words that immediately spring to mind when we think 'angel'.

Wings
Halo
Flying
White
Singing
Harp
Clouds
Goodness
God
Heaven
Demon
(yes, that's right; demon. More of this later.)

OK, we could go on for a while.

Douglas Bader • *Elvis* • *Grace Darling* • *Rosa Parks*

For centuries, the stereotypical angel has been the figure that appears in religious art, most notably in the gorgeous paintings of Italian artist Fra Angelico; the winged, haloed, floaty-gowned, androgynous, beautiful figures that appear somewhere up in the clouds, maybe pointing towards earth, perhaps plucking a harp or blowing a trumpet to suggest the glory of God. Then there are the angels depicted in films: Clarence, the angel in Frank Capra's lovely film *It's A Wonderful Life* appears as a sweetly eccentric, cherub-faced old gent. Luc Besson's *Angel-A* shows us a tall, svelte, seductive catwalk model, a real sauce-pot. In truth, the idea of the angelic being beamed down to fix things for us faulty and misguided human beings down on Earth has provided scope for a zillion interpretations on the theme, and is reflected in countless images in films, paintings, sculpture, poetry, literature. In truth, the idea of the angel is a fundamental part of our psyche whether we like it or not.

Putting artistic license to one side for the moment, what exactly IS an angel? In order to understand what we're dealing with in this book, let's see if we can nail some kind of an explanation.

The trusty *Encyclopaedia Britannica* is as good a place as any to look for guidance. Of course, this isn't the place to reproduce the entire article; we're only looking for a pointer. It is interesting to note that there's no entry simply for 'Angels', but only for 'Angels and Demons'. More of this later. Here are the first few sentences from the entry:

'ANGELS. The term angel, which is derived from the Greek word *Angelos,* is the equivalent of the Hebrew word *Mal'akh,* meaning "messenger". The literal meaning of the word angel thus points toward the function or status of such beings in a cosmic hierarchy rather than toward connotations of essence or nature, which have been prominent in popular piety, especially in Western religions. Thus, angels have significance in what they do rather than what they are.'

Interesting. Here, there's no mention of God, or of the angel being a creature of divine purpose. But then, the writer has already warned us that this is a very literal translation. A postman is the best example I can think of a messenger. Would we call the postman an angel, then? With due respect to postmen all over the world, and with exceptions, probably not! The last sentence from the entry is the telling one; 'Thus, angels have significance in what they do rather than what they are'; so in this instance, it would be the actions of the postman that would elevate him from the realms of ordinary messengers.

We'll see during the course of this book that as soon as we try to analyse the nature and appearance of an angel, we're met by a mass of contradictions, despite the series of clues that are a part of our generic knowledge of such creatures. They are large, small; benevolent, fearsome; peaceful, vengeful. And of course, they can be 'light' or 'dark'.

In addition, there are thousands of them. Billions, if it's true that every single person has a guardian angel, although this concept is never expressed definitively in the Bible. In fact, in searching for angels the Bible is by no means the first port of call. Although they are mentioned extensively in both Old and New Testaments, they're hardly ever given names. You'd be better placed to start with the Qur'an, since belief in angels is fundamental to the Islamic faith.

Gustav Davidson's wonderfully comprehensive *A Dictionary of Angels* catalogues an awe-inspiring number angels by name, and admits to having had to 'weed out' very many of the obscure ones about whom the author could find no specific information.

Marco Polo • *Alex Maiolo* • *Stanley Meyer* • *Nikola Tesla*

It seems, too, that in order to understand the nature of angels, we have to reject all our knowledge of conventional physics and embrace, instead, the quantum kind. Angels can be as huge as the planet at the same time that several thousands of them were said to be able to dance on the head of a pin; teasingly, this is likely to be the very same pin that we are trying to stick these angels with!

When I started writing this book, I met a very wise lady, Antoinette. Antoinette is the best-selling author of several cookbooks, and gained her audience most notably when she wrote extensively about specialist dietary requirements. A major supermarket stocks her branded range of foods. She lives in a beautiful house in the English countryside, surrounded by beautiful gardens that edge onto a wilder rural idyll. In addition to her writing, Antoinette is a Reiki master who also uses flower essences in her work, and freely admits her regular contact with, and help by, angels and angelic energies.

Antoinette told me that as soon as I started to look into angelic energies, these energies would start to manifest, but not necessarily in the form that I might expect. It makes sense to suppose that, if angels need to appear to us, they certainly wouldn't want to alarm or frighten us. It's also reasonable to imagine that, since you have picked up this book, you have chosen to open yourself to the possibility of these energies, too. So, in order to recognise these energies for what they actually are, try to put aside any expectations and simply start to see what happens.

Here's a fabulous story about the appearance of an angel. It's told by Bronwyn Bunt, whom I first met in her incarnation as rock-chick supremo, manager of several Detroit garage bands and founder of fashion label Made in Detroit. It was only when I got to know her better that her extensive knowledge of the

Lynne Lauren • Tylluan Penry • Bill Gates • Warren Buffett

Kaballah emerged, and I realised that there was way more beneath the surface of this sensationally-beautiful former model than I could have ever realised. Her letter is so fascinating that I'm reproducing it here in full.

Bronwyn's Angel

'I do have several personal experiences with angels. The explanation I would have given at the actual occurrence of the experience is vastly different from the explanation that I would give now, but they were most definitely angelic encounters, and the only thing that has changed is my definition of what an angel actually is.

'I was raised in an extremely fundamentalist Christian sect. As a child I loved it – I went to church as often as I could, I attended church camp, I was an active participant in Sunday school and church functions. When I was 12 we started our first classes towards missionary training. To cut a long story short, I discovered inconsistencies in the teachings that were so devastating to me that I felt betrayed by every adult that I knew and trusted. I felt they had all been lying to me, because if I, at the age of 12, could see that this stuff was fake, then the grown-ups must have certainly known. So I became an atheist (and very outspoken about it) at that early age.

'When I was 18, in the spirit of breaking out of my small town sheltered life a bit more, I agreed to drive my girlfriend to Iowa to see her boyfriend's band playing on New Year's Eve. Mind you, I drove a rusted-out Maverick that I had purchased for $75. It had four bald tyres, no heat, no radio and we were driving through four Northern states at the end of December. Needless to say we got not one, but two flat tyres just outside of Chicago. Now, I had never been to a major metropolitan city before. All I knew of

Prof Alan Jones • *Phillip Carr-Gomm* • *Stephanie Carr-Gomm*

them was what I saw on the news, which translated into one simple truth – if you go to a large city you will be raped and murdered. I know differently now, but at the time I was *sure* that I would be raped and murdered if I want to a large city. Lucky for me we just needed to drive through Chicago, not stop there…and then the tyres blew. Both of us were scared to death. The sun was just setting, we were freezing, we had one bald spare in the boot and didn't have any way of reaching anyone. Our only choice was to step out of the car and try and flag someone down. Neither of us could muster the courage to do it. I was crying, she was crying – so I prayed. It was kind of a pissed off prayer, but I seriously prayed hard for the first time in six years. I just wanted to live. As I was praying a small blue car pulled onto the hard shoulder behind us. I was expecting to see an axe murderer, but instead a young girl with mousy brown hair stepped out of the blue car and knocked on our window. (I'm cutting a longer story short here!) Her name was Jenny Brown (exactly the same name as my sister), and she drove us around trying to find an open service station to repair the tyres. When the service station wouldn't accept our cheque as payment, she paid. She let us sit in her warm car while they put the new tyres on our car and then drove away, even refusing our offer of repayment.

'It seems like a simple, even silly event, but it had such a profound effect on me. What is the classic definition of an angel? A messenger of God. So in the context of that definition, that simple act of kindness and selflessness was actually the delivery mechanism of a message that I needed to hear – that there is a God and I'm going to be alright.

'My definition of "God" has evolved since then, but at that moment and time, Jenny Brown – whoever or whatever she was – provided the perfect delivery mechanism for a message that I needed to hear, delivered by an "angel".'

Yuri Gagarin • *Buddy Holly* • *Ennio Morricone*

So, here's an example of help arriving from an unexpected quarter. But it's interesting to note that this aid doesn't come unbidden. Bronwyn says she '...prayed hard for the first time in six years', and we might suppose that her early upbringing in the fundamentalist faith in her early years would have given her a deep-seated belief in the power of prayer, despite her later rejection of that same faith. We might also suppose that her atheism was a reaction to the lies she felt that she'd been told, and not in fact the wholesale rejection of a Supreme Being that atheism actually implies. We'll see later in this book that it's important not to throw out the baby with the bathwater, to separate what works from what can be alienating or dogmatic.

David Lynch • *Amy Johnson* • *Donald Campbell* • *Amelia Earhart*

3

The Demon Dilemma

'He laughed, and I smiled in my trance. He showed me a closed
bag, then opened it and looked inside — but in such a way that I
could not see into it. Then a name came into my mind...'
— PAULO COELHO, *The Pilgrimage*

It would be impossible for me to write a book such as this, about angelic beings and energies, and choose to ignore the issue of demons. We'll see not only that one cannot exist without the other, but also that the way we popularly perceive the demon archetype could, in fact, be blinkered or misguided. The quotation above, from *The Pilgrimage* by Paulo Coelho, describes the moment when the book's protagonist meets his own personal demon for the first time — an essential part of his life's journey.

For a more pragmatic view of the subject, let's turn again to that stalwart, the *Encyclopaedia Britannica*, and see what it has to say.

'The term demon is derived from the Greek 'daemon' which means a 'supernatural being' or 'spirit'. Though it has been commonly associated with an evil or malevolent spirit, the term

John Morris   •   Ron Edwards   •   David Lynch   •   Henry Miller originally meant a spiritual being that influenced a person's character. An 'apathies daemon' ('good spirit'), for example, was benevolent in its relationship to men. Socrates, for example, spoke of his daemon as a spirit that inspired him to seek and speak the truth. The term was gradually applied to the lesser spirits of the supernatural realm who exerted pressures on men to perform actions that were not conducive to their well-being.

This brings us on to another crucial point in our analysis of the nature of the angelic. We need to be aware that some religions have been misused by people who sought a mechanism to control for masses by introducing a supernatural system of reward or punishment in the afterlife (the so-called heaven or hell). And we need to go back to the original meanings of terms such as 'angel' or 'demon' if we really want to know the truth. The 'fluffy' interpretations of angels that exist in various New Age emporia are part of the picture, certainly, but there's a far more profound and dichotomous side to our angelic beings and energies.

Our world is a balance of light and dark, necessary in a material environment. This is our environment, our home planet. As the sun rises out of darkness and sets into darkness, so the angel and the demon balance one another in a perfect cosmos. In order to understand one, we have to understand the other, and realise that 'good' and 'evil' exist only in the hearts and minds of mankind. Like electricity, energy is neutral. It's up to us to wield it in whichever way we choose, for good or bad, to heal or harm. It's this freedom of choice which separates us from the rest of the animal kingdom, and if we take the story of Adam and Eve (whether or not we believe it's a parable or the actual truth) then we see that they elected to use that freedom of choice when they partook of the Fruit of Knowledge, even though they had been warned that doing so would lead to death..

Doug and Joy • *Ellen Macarthur* • *Jont* • *Oppenheimer*

As the Reverend Doctor Clive says in the foreword to this book, it's as well to recognise that our angelic energies are older than any of our organised religions. Angels were here long before we gave them names or tried to rationalise them by categorising and making them fit into convenient boxes. They were here before mankind sorted them into teams of 'good' and 'bad' or 'black' and 'white'.

It's possible that the most frightening demons are not from the supernatural realms at all, but are the ones that are inside us.

Freud • Jung • You • Picasso • Lyn and Margaret Regan

4

Angels of the Dark Side

Did they fall, or were they pushed?

To understand Angels one must also understand demons and devils. These are more common and can be found in numbers through the valleys of South Wales and beyond. And all over the entire world, indeed! Paul Lewis came to save me from alcohol and an aversion to opening envelopes, all the way from the Isles of Scilly. I consider him one of my angels. I have other ideas of angels which are my three horses. They have taken me from bad things to some of the best times of my life. Importantly, some things we have done together have been life threatening, like racing over jumps. But the bond, being so strong, made me feel like I was on the back of angels, because they took care of me. I also took care of them. Am I one? I think it's obvious that there is demon and angel in all. And they are all around us, too. It is like beauty being in the eye of the beholder.

— BRYCHAN LLYR

Me • Ptolemy • JK Rowling • JRR Tolkien

In the same way that we looked at the archetypal idea for angels, let's do the same for demons. Here are some of the suggestions that people made:

Dark
Evil
Wings, but different to those of angels –
'...more like leathery bat wings'
Liable to trickery
In a war with angels which they will always lose
Were originally good but went bad
The product of God, just like angels

Essentially, we have here a creature which has many of the qualities of an angel, yet, it seems, with a diametrically opposed personality. The story about how, after God created the world, he asked angels to bow down before mankind and the best and brightest of them all – Lucifer – refused to kow-tow and so started a war in Heaven, is well-known. It's not surprising that such an epic tale has inspired literature, cinema, comic books, art.

Bearing in mind the overarching belief that a Supreme Mind is behind all the machinations of the universe, we have to ask ourselves whether the demons that stalk our earth and haunt the innermost recesses of our psyche are also fulfilling a purpose which is ultimately for the greater good. We've already discussed the notion that it was the 'fallen' angels that imparted the gifts of healing, music and prophecy to mankind.

Is it possible that these 'fallen' beings of light were deliberately pushed? And do demonic energies exist in the same way that angelic ones do? Undoubtedly. But just like angels, demons don't always manifest in the way we might expect.

Here's something that happened to me a few years ago. I was

Pablo Casals • Jaqueline DuPrey • Maria Callas • Carl Sagan

doing PR for a band which was recording its album in a fabulous studio just outside of London. The studio was based in and around a very beautiful old house. This house was without doubt the most haunted buildings I had ever come across, and I've never found anything like it since. In fact, it's where I met my husband, and one of the first conversations we had was about the ghosts in this place. The feeling there wasn't at all frightening, but joyful and cheeky. I can remember one particular moment standing in the lovely, huge old kitchen. There were only a half a dozen or so 'real' human beings in the room, but it felt as though there were 30 more at least, all there to enjoy the party.

I loved doing music PR. It was fun working with creatively-inspired people who were happy for me to be as lateral as I wanted to be. The band in question, Natural Life, were up for absolutely anything and then some, and so I returned to the house with the band's manager, an infrared photographer, a journalist, and a spiritual medium.

After spending an interesting few hours communicating with the spirits that inhabited the house and taking photographs of them, it was after midnight and we'd visited every room except for one off the main hall, which was always kept locked. We'd noticed the room earlier in the day and we were told that it had a weird atmosphere, so no-one used it. Now, anywhere else, describing a room as having a 'weird atmosphere' would have been acceptable, but don't forget that this house is already very, very strange. I knew that Mark, the medium, was intrigued, and so was I. As soon as the journalist, the manager and the photographer had retired into the kitchen to have coffee, I got the key from behind the reception desk and we unlocked the room.

It was a relatively small room compared to the scale of the rest of the house, maybe a bit bigger than an average-sized living room.

Jonathan Cainer • Dame Margot Fonteyn • Nureyev • The Heathies Ghandi

What was curious is that everything in the room was off-white, and didn't look as though it had been touched since the early '70s. The walls were white, the drawn curtains where white, the curvy leather corner-suite sofas were white. There were two low white coffee tables. The carpet was white. The whole effect was strangely grubby and disturbing. It seemed odd that the room hadn't been redecorated in keeping with the rest of the house.

'Right,' said Mark. 'There's work to be done it here. This might be the most important part of the whole day.'

Then he closed the door to the room with us both in it. He told me to stand in front of the door and hold out my hands and to 'just send out light'. I asked when, and why? But Mark said I'd know when and why.

Feeling a little freaked, I did as I was told. Mark snapped off the light and walked into the middle of the room, facing the corner to the left of the fireplace.

Although it seemed to be pitch dark, after a short while it was possible to make out the shapes of the furniture. I could see Mark's outline – arms outstretched, facing the corner of the room, praying.

And there was something in the room that I hadn't noticed in the sharp overhead light. In the corner, the corner that Mark seemed to be concentrating on, was a dark, crouching shape. As I watched, the shape started to grow…and I'm afraid I chickened out, snapped on the light and ran out of the room. As I was standing in the hall, trembling, Mark came out. He was perspiring. 'Look', he said, 'This thing can't hurt you while I'm there, but we have a chance to send it away, and I can't do it on my own. Come back into the room. You can put your hand on the doorknob if you want to and leave any time you like. All I need is for you to stand there and send out light towards the thing that's in the room. I know you can do this.'

• *Stephen Hawking* • *Mother Teresa* • *Peter Sellers*

So I steeled myself and went back into the room with Mark. We took up positions as before; me by the door (but *not* holding the handle!) and Mark in the centre of the room facing the corner.

Lights out. It began again.

The dark shape gradually grew and as it did, Mark's praying gathered in intensity. I found that, effortlessly, light was pouring from me, not just from my hands but from all of me; it was as though I was acting as a hose for some kind of cosmic emanation, and the tap had been turned on full. And I found that I had no fear, not even when the all-absorbing darkness was as high as the ceiling and starting to curl across it like a huge cobra made from black smoke.

I could also see that there was an enormous halo of light surrounding Mark, whose praying had reached a fever pitch. Suddenly, 'Phoof!' the dark cobra fizzled extremely rapidly back down into the corner, seemingly into the floor, and disappeared. At the same instant Mark collapsed onto the floor, and I stood for a few moments longer enjoying the sensation of the light, which gradually diminished in intensity. Then I turned, opened the door, and helped Mark up and out of the room. He was shaking and sweating, absolutely drenched in perspiration. I sat him down and went to get some water.

When he was feeling better, we went back into the room, and sat on one of the sofas to talk about what had happened. The atmosphere in the room was utterly different; I'd describe it as being lighter, lifted. The dark, grubby energy was completely dispelled, and Mark congratulated me on taking part in my first exorcism.

What was that energy? Was it something demonic, from the nether regions of the Underworld, the dark bowels of the Earth? Yes and no.

We subsequently found out that the house had belonged, in

Tony Benn • *Joanna Lumley* • *Keir Hardie* • *T E Lawrence*

the '70s and '80s, to a very famous rock musician. It was around about the time that people were doing lots and lots of drugs – real class A stuff including cocaine and heroin. It was apparently in this small, dank, white room that most of the drug-taking took place.

Now, I don't know if you've ever been around many people who use these sorts of hard drugs on a habitual basis. With some people, you can almost smell it, and it can make them, irritable and bad tempered. It's extremely addictive for some, and can give delusions of grandeur and an artificial feeling of well-being and euphoria which lasts only as long as the hit, making people crave more.

I wonder if it's possible that the dark, dense tower of 'demonic' energy which towered above us, cobra-like, was the result of all the 'bad' energies deposited into this room by the people in it, who altered their state by taking some seriously toxic and psychically-disturbing substances?

Is it possible that other instances of the things that we call demonic energies could actually emanate from human beings?

Richard Burton • *Finlay, Janette and Tyler* • *George Harrison*

5

The Angel
of Mons

Highlighting a Dilemma

I n September 1914, a London-based newspaper called *The
Evening News* published a story by Arthur Machen. As well as
being a factual reporter for the paper, Machen was – and still is –
a well-known writer of fiction in the gothic/supernatural genre.

This patriotic short story was entitled *The Bowmen*, and told
how supernatural forces had come to the aid of the British army
during a particularly difficult campaign. Tellingly, the story was
never actually labelled specifically as fiction, simply flagged by
the newspaper as 'Our Short Story'. To set some context for
what happened, bear in mind that readers were used to
Machen's factual reportage, too.

Just a month earlier, on 22 and 23 August 1914, a battle took
place which, at such an early stage in the World War I, indicated
that perhaps the duration of the fighting might take longer than
had originally been anticipated. Indeed, the Battle of Mons was
a key incident, being the first significant defeat of German forces
by the British, which was something of a miracle in any case

Terry Gilliam • *David Lean* • *Michelangelo* • *Jim Morrison*

because the British forces were actually heavily outnumbered by the Germans on this occasion.

Whether or not the forces had otherworldly help during this particular battle, the legend of the Angels of Mons is arguably one of the most renowned stories of latter-day angelic intervention. Many people who don't know the Arthur Machen back story quote the example as evidence of the existence of angels; even without any knowledge of its context, accounts of what 'happened' are varied. Some say there were angelic beings sighted in the sky helping the British to drive off the enemy; other versions tell that the Germans also saw this invincible supernatural force and fled – an understandable reaction. We also have the possibility, rendered in some accounts, that the patron saint of England, St George, joined forces with the Archangel Michael to drive off the foe. Heady characters, indeed, to have on your side.

The problem is that even if there was any veracity in the sightings, the desperate eagerness, in view of world events at that time, to magnify and embroider any vestige of truth has rendered the whole incident extremely dubious, and it's also telling that despite the dedication of the many researchers and historians that have endeavoured to produced some actual evidence of the Angels of Mons or even a first-hand eyewitness report, this has proved an impossible task.

Machen's story seems to have come at a propitious time for the British, at least. The war was new and a frightening prospect, and existing soldiers, potential soldiers and the British public needed any reassurance they could get that the might and right of God was on their side. It's also likely that the troops themselves passed word around that celestial energies were effectively batting for the British team, as illustrated by a contemporary letter from Brigadier General John Charteris to his wife Noel, which reads as

Frank Capra • Yoav • Kelly Joe Phelps • Otis Redding

follows: '...then there is the story of the "Angels of Mons" going strong through the 2nd Corps, of how the Angel of the Lord on the traditional white horse, and clad all in white with flaming sword, faced the advancing Germans at Mons and forbade their further progress. Men's nerves and imagination play weird pranks in these strenuous times.'

The flames were fanned even further when, shortly after the publication of *The Bowmen*, several parish magazines approached Machen and *The Evening News*, asking permission to reprint the story. When he was asked for verification, Machen obviously refused, stating time and time again that the story was purely a fictional work of his own imagining. However, it seems that no-one wanted to hear this; in the preface to *The Bowmen*, Machen says: '...It seemed that my light fiction had been accepted by the congregation of this particular church as the solidest of facts, and it was then that it began to dawn on me that if I had failed in the art of letters I had succeeded, unwittingly, in the art of deceit. This happened, I should think, sometime in April, and the snowball of rumour that was then set rolling has rolled ever since, growing bigger and bigger till now it is swollen to a monstrous size.'

This whole incident of the Angels of Mons highlights a common difficulty where it comes to talking about angels, ghosts, any other sort of supernatural or otherworldly pheno-menon. Put simply, some people want so very much to believe in supernatural or divine forces that they don't look objectively at the actual evidence, preferring instead to grasp onto a comforting and self-serving fantasy. In the same way, a small lunatic fringe of conspiracy theorists give a bad name to serious researchers and investigators by their desperate longing to find evidence of sinister forces at work. As a result, any actual evidence of genuine conspiracy may be clouded in doubt and discredited, too.

The Buddha • Otis Redding • Neil Young • Jeff Beck

The experience of angels is an incredibly personal, subjective matter. To my knowledge, no-one has taken a definitive photograph of an angel; no-one has ever captured one on film. Because the experiences of angels is not 'normal', is outside the realms of common everyday experience, people often hold their stories close to themselves, not wanting to be judged as ditsy or prone to fantasy. Conversely, there are a great many people who are desperately keen to share their experiences, but this might not be for the right reasons.

Much of William Blake's imagery asks us to look at the world in a different way, and has a metaphysical approach. If we lived in a world where angels were seen regularly, and people talked openly about it, then some of the mystery would be taken away. Inevitably, we still tend to think in an empirical way. If we can't weigh it, measure it, or count it, if it won't fit in the box, it becomes problematic, stays on the fringes.

For me, this is a huge mistake. It's time to sort the wheat from the chaff, to try to understand what's behind the trash of the mass-manufactured Chinese trinkets that pass for angels in many quarters. But we can't afford to dismiss anything; what if the stuff that some might regard as trash actually carries a great meaning for some people?

The following story reminds us that we really can't afford to make any assumptions.

Marie's Story

'I am 62 years of age and been an avid reader and follower of all forms of the spirit world ever since I was a teenager. I've learned a lot during this time and although I do firmly believe in angels, I've never had the sort of experience like the ones that some people claim to have had, of a beautiful being that appears before

Carlos Castenada · *David Attenborough* · *Brian Eno* · *Peter Gabriel*

them. But maybe that's because I've never asked for such an apparition, or maybe I've never needed to have one. Regardless of that, I still believe in them. I think the experiences that I have had are a little different to the gorgeous angels that seem to be seen by lots of people, therefore they seem to be a bit more down to earth and realistic, if that's the right word! I think it's good that people might think about finding Angels in more normal circumstances as opposed to the ones that are filled with light and mystery.

'For many years I've been a practitioner of something called Spirit Rescue. This all started a little while after the Chernobyl disaster happened. I awoke in the middle of the night to see the presence of a very large man, in what looked like a kind of uniform, standing by my bed. The uniform was either black or a very dark navy blue colour.

'I was taken aback; seeing a strange man in a uniform standing by the bed isn't a regular occurrence for me! But I talked to the man with my mind, telling him that I'd help him and giving him advice as to what he should do, given that he was, quite literally, a lost soul.

'It wasn't anything that I would have expected, but from that point onwards many more lost and frightened spirits were brought to my attention in various ways, so over the next few years I just carried on doing what I had to do, instinctively and automatically.

'What I did notice is that many of the spirits I was dealing with were soldiers or otherwise from the military – not always, but quite often.

'I should also mention that, like many people, I have a "parking guide" who always directs me to a parking place! He's called Major Tom; I realised that Tom must be directing these people to me because he's a military man, too.

'A few years passed, and one year I was on holiday in

Bob   Geldof   •   Bono   •   John   Martyn   •   Chrissie   Hynde

Arundel, a lovely town, about a month after Christmas. I walked into a small but beautiful shop filled with lots of gifts and trinkets and unusual items – you know the sort of thing. In the front of the shop was an Angel figure made of clear plastic, about 12" high with a light fitted inside that made the figure glow with incandescent colours. Lovely, I thought; he must be left over from the Christmas decorations; the snow around his feet and the reduced price were a bit of a give-away!

As I turned away to carry on browsing, I suddenly heard a voice say, "I AM THE ANGEL OF MONS".

'I stopped in my tracks and looked around, realising that, yes, this probably WAS how that particular angel might have looked. Well, the angel obviously wanted my attention so I bought him and now have him in my bedroom, where I have an idea that he helps to guide these lost souls to me, all those poor men who have lost their lives in battles of one sort or another.

'I also use angel visualisations to protect my family, especially when they are far away from home. I use the same visualisations when people are vulnerable or in need of guidance.

'The funny thing that was shown to me is that when I use angels in their guise as guardians, they don't have wings. I was actually stopped mid-way though a visualisation to be hugged by a being that had hair to about a couple of inches above his shoulders. He was wearing the sort of upper body type covering worn by Roman soldiers, and I knew instinctively that this was someone that I had known from some other time'.

Now, whether the Angel of Mons existed or not, or was a work of fiction, doesn't really matter that much. Whatever the case, its impact has been profound, and the very idea of such a being has become a common currency for us. It has become a part of our language.

Brancusi • George Best • Pele • Django Reinhardt • Sherpa Tensing

It's my aim in writing this book to have a more open approach to the energies that we call 'angelic'; not to render them ordinary, but in being able to accept the possibility that, as Marie points out, they really are more common than we realise, and to allow us to regard ourselves as more extraordinary than we had thought.

And I'll leave you with a possibility:

What if angelic forces themselves were behind the mass acceptance, at a time when reassurance was needed, of the story of the Angel of Mons?

Alexandra David-Neal • *Miles Davis* • *David Tomlinson*

6

Do I have to be a Christian to Believe in Angels?

No, you certainly don't. In fact, I think that a fervent belief in any one dogma, to the exclusion of anything else, is unlikely to enhance our experience of life in general, let alone our spiritual life in particular. Belief in both angels and demons extends way beyond the reaches of Christianity, and although they might take on different forms and go by different names, the concept of winged messengers from God, or indeed the Gods, is a collective part of our human psyche and completely outside the bounds of any one single religion. That's not, of course, to say that angels don't exist for anyone that's passionate about the Christian faith. Many of the current iconic images of angelic beings have their roots in Christian art and so it's inevitable that they might present to us in a way that's familiar, despite – or because of – our personal beliefs.

In the same way that we have a mutually acceptable idea of how an angel should be, we have a similarly universal idea of the appearance of a demon. These demons did not always start out

David McAlmont • Glenn Miller • Danny Kaye • Chi Fi Masters

as 'baddies', though; indeed, a good example is the horned nature god, Pan, whose cloven hoofs, tail, horns, salacious reputation, and his love of wild places, all became identified with the Devil himself. As with any powerfully repetitive thought form, the very fact that these 'evil' creatures were invented now means that many people see, feel and experience them as being very real indeed.

Mark's Story

Mark Townsend's background is very interesting and unusual. He's still a reverend in the Anglican Church but his life took a very different turn relatively recently when the questions that he was asking became too difficult for the elders in his particular church to deal with. Mark has now been initiated as a Druid and embraces the Pagan philosophies wholeheartedly whilst seeing very clearly that there are many beautiful ways that Christianity and Paganism can co-exist. He leads non denominational services and combines his love of stage magic (he's a member of the Magic Circle) with real magick – the supernatural kind, the kind that's sometimes, thanks to Aleister Crowley, differentiated by the use of that final 'k'. Here's his story.

'We were two very enthusiastic Pentecostal teenagers…I'll call my chum "Alvin". We were all set to go and stay down in my family beach hut on Mudeford Sandbank, near Bournemouth. The trip down was long, long, long and very boring. I remember us trying to pass the time away by listening to Jimmy Swaggart preaching tapes (see, we really were keen!). We were his number one fans in those days. Oh how things change – couldn't imagine Swaggart dancing round Stonehenge with me and my Druid mates!

'But Alvin and I then started talking about spiritual and

Gustave Klimt • Gustave Holst • Vaughan Williams • Stravinsky miraculous stuff. I think the preaching tape had prompted something or other. We started talking about angels and, as time ticked on, we became convinced that we would "meet" an angel (or more) during this beach hut holiday. It was October 1987 – in retrospect, a pretty stupid time of year to go and stay on a beach.

'I can't remember what we did while we were down there, but I can remember the last night. In fact, it's something I'll never forget.

'It was the night of the infamous 1987 hurricane...a hurricane that swept up the breadth of England from the south coast, ripping off house roofs and tearing down trees as it swirled and growled and breathed its way up the country. And we were on a beach near Bournemouth...in a wooden hut.

'That night we sat in the hut peering out – with a mixture of excitement and fear – at the harbour that was getting rougher, and higher, and scarier. Boats had broken free from their moorings, and stuff was flying around in the wind. Neither Alvin nor I – nor many other people in the UK, I suppose – realised the true seriousness of the situation. I remember being glued to the front window and watching the madness – we both occasionally pointed out and asked, "Is that the angel?". I can't say that either of us saw one but the next morning, when we opened the door and walked out onto the beach, we both freaked and came to the same conclusion – the night before was worse, more dangerous, than we'd assumed...and we were safe. We were safe because we'd been looked after. The fact was that our hut was one of the undamaged ones – in fact; it was the ONLY undamaged one. We finally walked to the bus stop and took a ride into town. Roofs ripped off, trees knocked down, and radio reports of hurricanes. "Shit! Looks like we did meet angels!", we said. Well perhaps not "Shit." After all, we were Pentecostals.'

Beethoven   •   Heinrich Biber   •   Rudolf Steiner   •   Paganini

A Short Note about Time

The other thing to bear in mind is just how important it is to remember that time is NOT linear, and that our way of measuring it in this way is nothing but a handy device. If there are such things as angels and angelic energies, then we need to look beyond external appearances, even the ones promulgated by Christian-based art, since as we'll see their form changes according to fashion and belief. How else, for example, would an angel be able to be in many different places at once? If we're going to be working with angels, then it's a good idea to find out how to recognise them. In this next section we'll try to find the component elements that belong to angels, no matter where or when they are from.

Carlos Santana • *W B Yeats* • *William Blake* • *Ted Hughes*

7

A Brief History
of Angels

Now, this might require a stretch of the imagination, but historically speaking, the very first image that bears any similarity to an angel dates from six thousand years ago, from the Naquada period of pre-dynastic Egypt. The image, commonly known as the Dancing Goddess, shows a creature which appears to be a bird/woman hybrid, arms curled up over her head in a position that suggests wings. Bear in mind that she appears 2,500 years before the Exodus of Moses and the Children of Israel, and you get some hint of the profoundly important part that the angel symbol has to play in our subconscious minds. In further answer to the question that heads the previous chapter, it's worth stating once again that the iconography of the angel existed long before Christianity, and Christianity certainly does not have a monopoly on these creatures; far from it. The gods and goddesses of Ancient Egypt, too, all appear with wings, often as human/animal hybrids.

Let's take a quick snapshot of what various faiths and philosophies believe about angels.

Virginia Woolf • *Mo Mowlam* • *Einstein* • *Debussy* • *Mozart*

Greek and Roman Angels

The images of angels that we're familiar with were actually 'recycled' from portraits of the gods and goddesses of the Ancient World. Those ubiquitous wings, again, are a symbol of the connection with the divine, an ability to transcend the earthly, material realms in favour of the spiritual. The cute, chubby winged figures that appear often in Christian art have their origins in the Roman figure of the earlier pagan god, Cupid, who was depicted as a winged child. These particular figures – called '*putti*' – are technically not actually angels at all. Although we sometimes refer to them as 'cherubs', this is incorrect; real Cherubim are far more grandiose creatures.

The Romans also subscribed to the belief about a sort of guardian spirit. For the man, this was called the 'genius' and for the woman, 'juno'. We'll see that this idea also has parallels in many different beliefs.

Sumerian Angels

Here, we find an iconic angel figure known as the Angel of Nimrub, which dates back to 875BC. You're probably familiar with this distinctly male figure, his profile facing to the right, with two sets of rather grandiose wings. Earlier angels might all be human/animal/bird hybrids, but the wings are a constant. It was likely to be the Sumerians that gave us the idea that angels were the 'sons of God' who found earth women so alluring that they flew down here to mate with them, which is described in Genesis Chapter 6. The resultant children grew into the terrible gigantic creatures called the Nephilim, the equivalent of demons, who were handily blamed for all the miseries and woes of the world. The Sumerians believed that the angels – or '*igigi*'

Capability Brown • Frank Lloyd Wright • Norman Foster

– were both messengers between man and his gods, and also ministers of the gods. It seems that the idea of the 'dark' counterpart of the angel is as old as the hills; the malevolent flipside here were called 'anuna-ki' who lived underneath the earth itself. Here, we see once more the idea that 'up there' in the heavens is the realm of the good, whilst 'down there', beneath the material world, lurks evil.

The Babylonians

Taking over the rulership of Mesopotamia after the Sumerians from 1850 – 900BCE, the Babylonian equivalent of the *igigi* as divine messenger, or angel, was the *sukall'*. The role was the same: to pass on messages from above to below and back again, and to act as divine servants of the gods. Note here that we're still saying 'gods'.

There are two key Gods from this time, Ba'al and El, who were extremely antagonistic towards one another. It seems that El became the equivalent of the jealous 'One God' who gains increasing prominence during the next few thousand years of Judeo Christian and Islamic history, and so it makes sense that Ba'al was, quite literally, demonised. It is interesting to note that it is the name of this early God, El, who gives us the suffix that appears at the ends of the names of many of our angels and archangels.

Zoroastrianism

This is a fascinating system of belief from ancient Persia, which is now known as Iran. The tenets of the faith were dictated to Zoroaster (Zarathustra), the sage, magician and miracle-worker who lived between 627 and 551BCE and, like other key religious

Joan of Arc • Jimmy Page • Jimi Hendrix • Robert Plant

figures, seems to have stirred up trouble by asking difficult questions of those in authority. In Zoroastrianism we find the forerunners to the seven immortal beings that are compared to the archangels, and indeed provides much of the historical context for many of the commonly-held beliefs about angels in the Judeo-Christian tradition. These seven 'original' angels are called the *Amesha Spentas*, meaning 'bounteous immortals'. Each of the seven represents a different facet of the nature of the Supreme Creator, in the same way that the innumerable Hindu deities are all facets of the one Divine Being.

Zoroastrianism also encompasses the concept of the guardian angel, or *Fravashi*. Zoroastrians believe that every single human being has his or her own *Fravashi* which assists the individual from the moment of birth until the moment of death. Again, a universally-accepted idea.

And once more, each of the seven *Amesha Spentas* has its shadow counterpart. The most powerful of these, the leader, is called Ahriman, the Lord of Darkness. Ahriman has at his command the *Devas*, or devils.

Angels in Islam

'Every raindrop that falls is accompanied by an angel,
for every raindrop is a manifestation of being'
—THE QUR'AN

The Islamic word for 'angels', *Malaikah*, is similar to the Hebrew word, *Mal'akh*, which as we've discovered, means 'messenger'. The Judeo-Christian belief in angels closely resembles the pattern set out in the Qur'an, which states that every person has not one but two guardian angels assigned to him or her; one to record all the good deeds, and the other to

Josh Homme • Kurt Cobain • David Bowie • Frank Sinatra

record the bad. (The concept of the guardian angel is only hinted at in the Bible, never clearly stated). The similarities between the Judeo Christian angels and the Islamic ones goes further, since both traditions believe that the four throne bearers of God, or Allah, are represented by a man, a lion, a bull and an eagle.

Belief in angels is a crucial tenet of Islam. Whereas there's some debate in the Old Testament of the Bible as to whether angels were invented before or after mankind, the Qur'an states that they were created from pure light prior to the creation of humankind. We're also told that angels are beautiful and have wings, and also that they have specific messages to bring, and roles to play, on Earth.

Unlike man, angels do not have free will, but are obliged to carry out the wishes of God. The Prophet Mohammed gives us a further definitive description of the angel: 'I have been given permission to speak about one of the Angels of God who carry the Throne. The distance between his earlobes and his shoulders is equivalent to a seven-hundred year journey.' (Abu Daud)

The credo taught by Mohammad, that every single aspect of the Earth has its own angel, is similar to the belief of animist faiths that everything has its own numinosity, or spirit, although it's unlikely that a fundamentalist might agree with this parallel.

The shadow side of angels is represented in Islam, too. Satan, the fallen angel, is found here under the name of Shaitan. In Islam, it is believed that he was cast out of Heaven because of his refusal to worship God's other creation, Adam. There's an anomaly here, given that we are also told that angels do not have the luxury of free will; presumably Satan was the exception. Demons are represented as Djinn, and whereas angels are said to be created of light, Djinn, also created, like the angels, before mankind, are exotically described as being made of 'smokeless fire'.

Bach • Carole King • W.M. Turner • Dali • Stubbs

The mysterious sect of Islam, Sufism, has an interesting idea about angels which stems from Zoroastrianism. On the journey to the Cinvat Bridge, a euphemism for the Otherworld, the soul is said to meet its destiny. This destiny is personified as a sort of angel-self or celestial soul. This 'angelic self' is the part of us that it is our task on Earth to find, and without whom our lives become meaningless and shallow. Here, the angel has a psychological role to play.

There's a latter-day Sufi master called Inayat Khan, who makes some very interesting points about angels. In his *The Soul, Whence and Whither* he tells us: '...every soul is an angel before it touches the earthly plane. The angels it is who become human beings; and those who do not become human beings, remain angels. The human being, therefore, is a grown up angel, or an angel whose soul has not grown sufficiently. Infants who come to earth with their angelic qualities and sometimes pass away without having experiences the life of the grown-up man, show us the picture of the original condition of the soul.'

Buddhism

When the mother of the Buddha became pregnant with her illustrious child, we read in the Buddhist Sutras that she was protected for the duration by four sword-wielding angels. This child went on to become the founder of the fourth largest religion in the world, and that's not including those who refer, I believe correctly, to Buddhism as a philosophy rather than a religion. Angels, for Buddhists, are equated to beings called *Devas*, about whom there are many theories. On the one hand there's a notion that they are beings that have been reborn for the benefit of mankind. Conversely, they could be beings that are unable to detach from the pleasures of the physical plane and so may never

Bunuel • *Terry Gilliam* • *Degas* • *Diaghilev*

attain the ultimate goal of Nirvana, or the eternal bliss of enlightenment. Others, in particular Tibetan Buddhists, say that the *Devas* are emanations of the Bodhisattvas, that is, those who have foresworn any idea of attaining their own enlightenment in the cause of staying here and helping others in their quest for salvation. This Tibetan belief stems from the pre-Buddhist cultures where the *Devas* show many qualities similar to that of the *Kami* of the Shinto faith, which we'll look at in a moment. Certain human beings can apparently attain Devahood after death. These specially-selected individuals would have to be the sort of be exemplary souls who manage to live a life of virtuous deeds and thoughts. The Buddha himself was reborn as a *Deva* prior to his final rebirth as the great leader we know him to be.

Hinduism

As organised religions go, Hinduism is one of the oldest. Its sacred texts, the Vedas, were written some 3500 years ago.

Hinduism can seem to the outsider like a confusing welter of gods and goddesses, but in fact these venerable deities are all facets of the multi-hued face of the overarching force for life, otherwise known as *Brahma*. Hindu culture doesn't give us angels as such, but rather has protecting and guiding spirits and entities whose functions are essentially the same as the creatures that we call angels. As well as the *Mahadevis* and *Mahadevas*, or the major deities such as Vishnu and Shiva, there are the inevitable entities that are lower in the celestial pecking order, called *Devas*. These *Devas* are spirits of nature, elementals that are connected to aspects of this planet, again similar to the *Devas* of the Buddhist belief and the *Kami* that appear in Shinto.

The word *Deva* actually means 'shining being' and it is believed that they are constructed of light – again, a quality of

Leonardo Da Vinci • Oscar Van Gelden • Chris Heywood • Galileo

the angel. The flipside of the *Deva* is the *Asura*, who is a similar creature but with a more mischievous or destructive bent.

The take on the role of this Hindu equivalent of the angel is probably quite pragmatic in many ways; for example, here we find beings called *Apsarses*, who are responsible for giving sensual pleasures to the gods. These angels occasionally come down to earth to perform the same function for man, and whilst doing so manage to curtail any evil thought or deed. Then there are the *Gandhrvas*, winged beings with musical skills enough to please both gods and men.

Incidentally, I witnessed something very curious when I was in India. I was at a Hindu temple, at a ceremony that was presided over by a very illustrious woman whose given name is Meenakshi. As I watched, her face was overcast by a beautiful greenish light. It didn't seem abnormal at the time – it was only in retrospect that I realised how strange it was. Later, I learned that the aspect of the goddess who is known as Meenakshi, and after whom this woman had been named, manifests with a greenish cast to her skin.

Shinto

Shinto is an ancient Japanese religion that has combined with Buddhism to form the most popular faith in modern-day Japan. We can't gauge its exact age, but it had certainly emerged by the 5th century BCE. It's an animistic faith, shamanistic in parts, with a fundamental reverence for the landscape and animals and a healthy interest in divination techniques

The Shinto equivalent of angels comes in the form of *Kamis*, spirits that rule over every aspect of life on earth. There are *Kamis* of the elements; of mountains; of trees, flowers, rocks. I'm reminded of the Islamic idea that 'every blade of grass has

Fra Angelico • *Alexander Graham Bell* • *Stravinsky* • *Magellan*

its angel'. Followers of Shinto believe that it's possible for human beings to become *Kamis* after death. Because every physical feature of the landscape - indeed, in the entire cosmos – is flowered into life by its own *Kami* which also inhabits it as a part of its life force, then it stands to reason that these physical objects are worshipped as sacred. There is no separation between the sacred and the mundane or profane, no dividing line here. Even families and clans have their own *Kami*, and intrinsic and essential part of the family.

Like angels, *Kami* are teachers, guides and protectors, aiding people towards the spiritual path wherever necessary. I can't help thinking that if we all regarded the planet in the way that the tenets of Shinto advise, then we wouldn't have the mess that we're currently looking at.

Judaism

The roots of Judaism and Islam are the same; both accept the teachings of the prophet Abraham. This same prophet forms the basis of Christianity, too. All three of these major patriarchal religions share many of the same theories about, and concepts of, angels, which in general stems from the Judaic teachings.

However, in Judaism the concept of the guardian angel doesn't exist; here, angels seem to have a very specific job, encountered undertaking the work of God on Earth. Angels should never be used by human beings as a sort of 'middle man' to get to God, says the Talmud; instead, rather than seeking angelic intervention, man should appeal directly to God.

Judaeo Christian belief tells us that angels, like mankind, were the creation of God. Any reader of the Bible with a particular interest in matters angelic might be confused at what seem to be gaps in the history of angels; this is because, where

Newton • Pythagoras • Boudicca. • Plato • Aristotle

there *are* gaps, these were once filled by writers of what's called the Pseudepigrapha, which are not accepted as genuine scripture. Nevertheless, some of the ideas contained in the Pseudepigrapha have taken root; for example, the idea that angels were invented on the very first day of creation, just after the heaven, earth and waters. Having said that, the book of Daniel describes how '....the heavenly beings shouted for joy....' when God created the initial infrastructure of the Earth; this gives a clue that perhaps the angels maybe were around before the Earth itself was made. However, this isn't the place to get carried away with such minutiae; we're looking here at form and ideas, with only a brief nod to what might or might not be interpreted as 'fact'.

As messengers from God go, the Angel Gabriel had a very profound role to play, advising of the imminent birth not only of Christ, but also of John the Baptist. In the Bible, too, we find that angels reveal their messages in the form of dreams and visions, which equate to many latter-day tales of angelic encounters, as we'll see throughout this book.

Judaism, like Zoroastrianism, puts seven major angels firmly at the core of the angelic belief system and it seems sensible to suppose that these 'Big Seven' are the same beings. Despite the teaching that man should appeal directly to God, these angels do actually mediate between God and man and vice versa. Their form is indeterminate, and has never been described as human in any writings.

Christianity

For good or bad, it tends to be the angelic beings from the Christian tradition that dominate, appearing on everything from the high art of the renaissance to the new age interpretations

Socrates • *Mary Magdalen* • *Blessed Virgin Mary* • *Brunel*

rendered in every sort of material from the sublime to the ridiculous.

The political infrastructure of Christianity is complex and labyrinthine, and it's fair to say that the simple philosophies of Christ have been obscured by centuries of infighting, and the unfortunate influence of those who have used religious observance as a means of social control and accumulation of wealth,

The Bible itself has been edited frequently, not surprising in a book of such antiquity, but what is curious is that some of the main information about angels has been removed. Specifically, the Book of Tobit describes the journey of Tobit and the Archangel Raphael, and interestingly, this is the only place where this important angel is mentioned by name. Raphael is one of the seven Archangels that relate to the seven *Amesha Spentas* of Zoroastrianism. The Book of Enoch, too, describes the angels that mated with human females to produce the monstrous giants called the *Nephilim*. This idea is symbolic of the heavens belonging to the beings of light, of spirituality, of the element of fire and the male, whereas our planet represents is the female, material world and the element of water and earth; literally, Mother Earth. It's as well to remember that these differing aspects are not good or bad, but complementary.

Elsewhere in the Bible, angels appear as guides, messengers from God, and with abilities to heal the sick. The angels that appear in the Bible, in accord with the patriarchal God that is said to have invented them, appear as male beings despite our general belief that angels are androgynous.

It would also appear from the Bible that angels can appear to be as solid as any human being, and we will think about this further later on. For example, in Hebrews Xiii, Chapter 2, we read '...*Do not forget to entertain strangers, for by doing so people have entertained angels without knowing it*'.

Marie Curie • *Louis Pasteur* • *Hypatia* • *Oracle of Delphi*

Many of the stories in this book feature angelic beings that pass for human; or does each human being have the spark of the angelic within them, ready to show itself when the moment is right?

The angels in the Bible, too, share other human attributes, capable not only of presumably eating and drinking, but of feeling happiness, sadness, joy, desire.

So, now we have a good snapshot of how angels manifest in some of the major faiths on this planet. It's interesting to see just how many close similarities there are.

It's probably not a surprise, given the emphasis that many religions place on angelic beings, that many people should encounter them in places of worship. Here's one such meeting.

Trish's Story

Trish is a dressmaker based in the north of England. She's a very down-to-earth, friendly woman, with a dry sense of humour and a passion for her job that's reflected in the huge collection of rare vintage wedding dress patterns that she has amassed. Before she started making wedding dresses Trish was a theatrical costumier.

'A couple of years ago I was employed make the wedding dress for a woman called Melinda. We clicked at the first meeting and the subsequent fittings got to be really enjoyable. We got to be such good friends that I was even invited to the wedding.

'There was going to be a rehearsal for the wedding at the church a couple of days before the Saturday wedding, and then a few of us were planning to go out for a meal. With a few others, I arrived at the church a bit earlier than Melinda and her prospective husband, Matt. I went for a bit of a mooch around the church, which was small, old, and very beautiful. I'm not a churchgoer and wouldn't even classify myself as a Christian to

Sir Christopher Wren • Laurence Olivier • Bronwyn Bunt • Dante

be honest but I do like churches, the colours, the statuary, the stained glass and the atmosphere.

'The vicar was a jovial chap and there was a lot of banter and laughter during the rehearsal, and a great, happy, excited feeling. As I watched, a strange thing started to happen. The space behind the altar started to get brighter and brighter, starting to spread to fill the entire area. I watched, mesmerised, partly wondering whether it was a light show of some kind. The light gathered itself together, sort of folded itself inwards, and as I continued watching it transformed itself into the form of what I can only describe as an angel, as big as the entire church wall behind the altar. I must have been sitting there with my mouth open. I looked around to try to gauge whether anyone else was seeing the same thing, but no-one was reacting; all eyes were on the bride and groom as they practised their vows.

'The angel didn't move; it was like a superimposed image, a 'still', if you like, rather than a film. And as gradually as it had appeared, it faded away'.

I asked Trish what the angel had looked like. Was it carrying anything, for example?

'It was bright! Hard to look at, but distinctly male; huge rays of light behind it that could I suppose have been taken for wings. Hands outstretched, not carrying anything that I noticed. It shimmered like light on water.'

I also asked if Trish had even experienced anything like this, either before or since.

'No. And I haven't ever mentioned it to anyone up until now, not fully. I did casually say to one of the people that were there with me that the church was unusually bright, but they didn't respond at all, so I can only assume that this wasn't a shared experience. The reason I haven't actually spoken about it is because, if someone had told me they'd seen this, I'd have

Lynne Lauren • *Chrissie G* • *Adam Fuest* • *Jack White*

thought they were mad. I wouldn't now, mind you. But I wouldn't want it known far and wide that I'd seen an angel, not really. People might think I was making it up, or fanciful, or something. But I do feel very, very lucky to have witnessed this, although I do wish it had been a shared experience. I know this might sound strange, but I wondered if this being showed itself in reaction to the joyful, happy feeling in the church that was caused by the excitement of the people that had gathered there from Melinda and Matt's wedding rehearsal.'

Lisa Johnson • Sarah Gregory • Einstein • Tania Ahsan

8

Let's Get Metaphysical

More technical stuff about angels

Inevitably, there's an academic side to Angelology, and as soon as we start looking into this we find what can appear to be quite a confusing and labyrinthine system of Principalities, Virtues, Orders, Angels, Archangels, Cherubim, Seraphim, etc. When we're talking purely about angelic energies, this system doesn't really matter, but for the purposes of clarity it's worth explaining a little of how this traditional way of categorising angelic beings actually works. As ever, though, there are ambiguities.

What we'll never know is whether this way of categorising different types of angels and explaining their ultimate relationship to one another and to mankind is actually real, or a human conceit, and again, it doesn't really matter. It might seem incongruous that cosmically-important celestial creatures would bother with what amounts to a pecking order – but that's exactly what it amounts to.

Another interesting point is that, despite the hundreds if not thousands of angelic names that we know about from various sources, only two angels are ever mentioned by name in the

Mark Townsend · Florence Nightingale · Roald Dahl · Ernst Haas

Bible, Gabriel and Michael. And even then, Michael is mentioned only in the New Testament.

Adding to the confusion is the array of differing opinions about the ranks and orders of angels, and their often-interchangeable names and functions. The fact that many illustrious spiritual and occult leaders have 'channelled' their own interpretations which are often at odds with one another has muddied the waters even further. Whatever the origins of this hierarchical system, the good news is that it all breaks down quite easily and there's a relatively simple explanation of how it is meant to work without needing to get too bogged down in what may, after all, still amount to a human conceit.

Much of what we accept in this area is down to the writings of early philosophers and thinkers, but it's true to say that the most popular current reasoning about the groupings of angels comes from Pope St Gregory who, in the 6th century CE, managed to unscramble the labyrinthine workings of the angelic world. He combined the Angels, Archangels, Cherubim and Seraphim mentioned in the Bible, with the grades of Angelic beings mentioned by St Paul; these are the Principalities, Powers, Virtues, Dominions and Thrones. Together, this makes nine 'orders' of Angels, and it's this system which the earlier acolyte of St Paul, known as Dionysius the Aeropagyte, had recorded in the first century CE after he heard St Paul preaching. When his identity was later called into question, the author was given the name 'Pseudo Dionysius' but whoever this writer was, he certainly had an impact on the way that we categorise angels. In a book called 'Celestial Hierarchies', he described St Paul's vision of Heaven which was arranged into nine orders – also known as 'Choirs' – orbiting God's throne. Pseudo Dionysius divided them thus:

Ansel Adams · Simone Johnson · Alan Card · Mike H · Judika Illes

Seraphim, Cherubim and Thrones
Dominions, Virtues and Powers
Principalities, Archangels and Angels

There are further divisions within these groups, and we'll look at these next.

Essentially, the nine groups have further bundles of three within them. These groups spiral around a central pivotal point of light, or the Godhead, transmitting light and power down from the Source (the 'top') to Man (the 'bottom'), while the entire collection forms part of a greater whole.

However, both the Islam and Judaism give us a different set of rankings. The latter list reads, from top to bottom, as: *Hayyoth ha'Qadesh* (meaning 'heavenly creatures'); *ophanim*; *erelim*; *hashmalim*; *seraphim*; *malakhim*; *elohim*; *bene elohim*; *cherubim*; *ishim*.

The Qur'an and the Hadith (the writings about the Prophet) give us the Islamic interpretation of the Hierarchies. These are as follows: Throne Bearers, (or *hamalat al-'arch*), Cherubim (*karibuyin*); Angels of the Seven Heavens; Guardian Angels; Attendant Angels; Journeying Angels (*sayahun*) and finally what are called 'Ordinary Angels'.

Although The Qur'an recognises four archangels, curiously, only two of these are named; Jibril (or Gabriel) and Mikha'il (or Michael). Traditional lore names the other two as Azrael and Israfel.

The Triads

According to Pseudo-Dionysius, creation emanates from the Supreme Being as pure light and pure wisdom. When we speak of the 'Higher Mind' that we are all a part of, it is this pure source that we mean, unadulterated truth and freedom from

All the contributors to this book • *James Lebon* • *Joni Mitchell*

worldly attachments. This energy flows down a sort of celestial helter-skelter to the first trinity of angels that are closest to the source. This first, and highest triad, is composed of the Seraphim, Cherubim and Thrones. This first triad represents God's ultimate perfection, supreme light and love.

This energy then flows to the second Triad, which represents the Supreme Being's dominion over creation; a power that is without limit and a force that cannot be resisted. The second trinity is comprised of Dominions, Virtues and Powers.

The final Triad is the one that is closest to our realm, the realm of humanity. This third group, of Principalities, Archangels and Angels, represents the external actions of God, i.e. government, revelations, and manifestations of an ultimately Divine benevolence.

Bear with me as we take a closer look at all these different vehicles of Angelic energy. Again, their provenance doesn't matter too much, but it's interesting to grasp the 'rules' since we have to assume that there's a reason for everything – even if we don't always understand it.

Seraphim

Otherwise known as Seraphs, these are the highest in the hierarchical ladder. The name is Hebrew and means 'Burning Ones'. We know relatively little about them, given that the only reference in the Bible describes them as having six wings, two of which cover their faces, two cover their feet, and a handy two are left with which to fly.

Cherubim

In legend, it was Cherubim that were sent by God to bar the gates to Eden after Adam and Eve left their own private little paradise. Although latterly Cherubim have been confused with the little

Rhona Heath · *Bobby Osborne* · *The Penponties* · *Lewis Carroll*

winged infants that are really called '*putti*' and are personifications of the pagan god, Cupid, real Cherubim are actually very fearsome creatures. It's likely that they are derived from the Assyrian '*karibu*', hybrid, winged spirits with the bodies of animals such as lions or bulls, wings like those of eagles, and the faces of human beings. Cherubim are further described in the Zohar as holding up the Universe, and Christian mysticism has them named rather poetically as Guardians of the Fixed Stars. They are also known as the Charioteers of the Divine Spirit.

Thrones

These are the actual chariots of that divine spirit. The names by which they are sometimes known, 'Ophanim' and 'Galgallim', also translate as 'wheels'. Ezekiel's vision describes them, quite surreally, as bright cosmic wheels with eyes all around the rims. You'll sometimes see pieces of art depicting these curious entities.

The Second Triad
Dominions

The first order in the second triad is called Dominions or Dominations. Pseudo-Dionysius referred to them as 'True Lords', and it is the Dominions – whose name stems from the same as the Latin for 'lords' – who inform the lower orders of angels of the orders and wishes of the Higher Power or Supreme Being. These orders are passed down from the Cherubim and Seraphim.

The order of the Universe is maintained by these Dominions, and they do apparently appear to human beings on extraordinarily rare occasions.

Virtues

The Virtues are the second part of this second triad, and they

Zoroaster • *John Dee* • *Nancy Palmer-Jones* • *Adam Fuest*

occupy the mid-point on the celestial ladder. Virtues are also called the Shining Ones and take care to regulate the Sun, moon, stars and planets as well as being responsible for the weather; rain, sun, wind, snow. It is the Virtues that give us courage.

Christ tells us that Virtues are also the guardian angels of children.

Powers

Here we come to some truly 'magickal' angels, one of the most intriguing groups of the lot, and the one which, in most likelihood, has the most to teach us.

Powers are the third of the second trinity. In true Star Trek fashion, these are named as the defenders of the universe, keeping the powers of evil away from humankind. They ensure that the souls of the dead reach Heaven safely, so inevitably the Powers tend to be associated with fate and destiny. Because of their dealings with such so-called 'dark' matters, the Powers themselves have also been associated with that same dark side. It stands to reason that any power capable of vanquishing evil must have some understanding of that evil in the first place, but this is something that we humans sometimes find a tricky theory to contemplate. In the world of the Powers, nothing is quite what it seems. Fortune telling, soothsaying or prediction of the future of any sort, under whatever guise, is associated with this order – as is the fear and superstition that sometimes surrounds such matters.

Legend tells us that the Powers were the first of the angels to be created, and it was from their order that the largest number of 'fallen angels' fell. It's interesting, too, to remember that legend tells us that Fallen Angels taught human womankind the skills of magic, prediction and healing. Arguably, these are all incredibly useful skills, and it raises the question; if everything

Jeanne McKenzie • Robert Atherton • Doreen Virtue • Jacqui Newcombe

in our perfect universe is pre-ordained, then did the Fallen Angels fall – or did they accept it as part of their destiny to come to Earth in this way, to teach us?

The leader of the powers is either Camael or Samael. Both are 'dark' angels, and Samael is sometimes described as the Angel of Death. Samael has also been named as the Antichrist, and again we have to think carefully about what this really means before we react to such emotionally-loaded words.

The Third Triad

This group is closest of all to the Human realms. Although the energy from the Divine Sources has spiralled downwards towards these angels who we perceive as being at the bottom of the rung, again, we need to suspend the normal mechanisms of our belief and get metaphysical, change the way we think about 'up' and 'down' – it's all a question of perspective.

Principalities

The first of this final three bodies of angels, Principalities, are said to be so huge and magnificent that they can never appear in any form whatsoever to mankind, and it is these Angels that are the guardians of religion, cities and nations. As the Powers have a dark side, so do the Principalities.

Archangels

These are the primary intermediaries between God and mankind. Pseudo Dionysius called them 'messengers that carry divine decrees'. Although archangels appear to be pretty low in the pecking order, this has some ambiguity, because they have a very close relationship with the Divine Spirit.

The seven angels, who, the Book of Revelation tells us, 'stand

Diana Cooper • The Prophet • Roald Dahl • Paulo Coelho

before the face of God' and that must relate to the seven celestial beings of the *Ahura Mazda*, are the seven archangels. These are named Michael, Gabriel, Raphael, Uriel, Chamuel, Jophiel and Zadkiel.

Michael is the 'boss' angel, the 'leader of the sons of light' and the 'viceroy of heaven'. Michael alone it is who remains uncorrupted by his close proximity to the Earthly Plane.

Ordinary Angels

Finally, the 'ordinary' angels are those closest to mankind, and act as intermediaries between humankind and the other angelic worlds. They have the power to protect us as individuals. It's safe to assume that the majority of 'guardian' angels would be recruited from this category.

Jesus Christ • Jeremy Clarkson • Patti Smith • Tim Smit

9

Do Angels Actually Exist?

'Be not forgetful to entertain strangers;
for thereby some have entertained angels unawares'

—HEBREWS 13:2

O K, so here's another odd chapter title; it would seem to be self-evident that a book with a title like this one would be fighting the corner of angelic energies and would therefore advocate their existence. But, as with all things angelic, it's not that simple.

Let's take a dangerous look at some statistics. And it IS dangerous, since you know what they say about 'lies, damn lies and statistics'! Statistics can be rigged to represent whatever people want them to depending on the questions asked and the people chosen to answer those very questions. Nevertheless, the following figures do raise some interesting questions.

A recent Gallup Poll survey, dated 2007, tells us that 75% of Americans believe in angels. Further, the Pew Poll survey which was carried out a year later tells us that seven out of 10 Americans believe that angels are active forces in the world. This breaks down further into differing religious groups:

Anita   Roddick   •   Alexandra   David-Neal   •   Dalai   Lama

78% of Jehovah's Witnesses believe in angels.
61% or Evangelical Protestants believe in angels.
59% of Mormons believe in angels.

However, the same poll tells us that 73% of Jews don't believe that angels are active in the world; 56% of Buddhists have the same belief, (or rather, the lack of a belief in active angelic powers in this world). And 54% of 'unaffiliated' people do not believe that angels are active in the world whatsoever.

Then there was another interesting survey carried out by Baylor University. The discoveries were as follows; that half of the American population believe that they're protected by guardian angels, twenty per cent believe that they've heard the voice of God actually speaking to them, 25% have witnessed 'miraculous' healings and 16% have received such a healing. This was a wide-ranging survey, with 1648 adults answering 350 questions. The conclusion reached by those who put the survey together is that the larger majority of people must be not only familiar with, but also can be presumed to be comfortable with, supernatural and mystical experiences. Either that, or, in the very extensive number of people questioned, the surveyors hit a rich vein of the insane, the delusional, and the attention-seeking. That's the beauty of such surveys; we'll never know. I have to say, though, that this seems unlikely.

And yet, particularly in the UK, I think, we still tend to separate these supernatural experiences out from 'everyday' experience in a way that is certainly not part of common practice in Eastern countries, where the material and spiritual worlds come together in a chaotic collision of statuary, music, offerings, incense and music. Are those 20% of the American population that believe they've heard the voice of God speaking

Barack Obama • *Jules Verne* • *Frances Drake* • *Dylan Thomas*

to them directly, liable to talk about it on the bus? Unlikely: they'd run the risk of certification if they did.

Why is that? Why, as the director of the survey points out, is the subject of angelic protection 'taboo' especially since the percentage of Americans who ascribe to atheism numbers only 4%?

Perhaps it's a congenital dis-ease in the West that we are unable fully to express the spiritual aspect of ourselves. Maybe we're afraid that people are going to think we're a bit 'ditsy'. I would suggest that this is changing, though.

But let's get back to the original question: do angels actually exist?

Some might dismiss angels as handy fictional characters from the Bible and other religious tracts that are able to step in and change things, give messages; in the theatre this is the 'deus ex machina', the 'god from the machine', a character or device that is dropped in at the last minute to solve the problem and wrap up the loose ends. However, there's also the argument that if we believe in something, then that belief alone is enough to 'prove' existence of anything at all. If everything starts as an idea – even something as rational and solid as a table, say – then it stands to reason that angels exist, whether real or as an idea, or even as an archetype. Further, there are thousands, if not millions of people, who believe that they have had direct experience of, or communication with, angels; for them, their direct experience means that their belief in angels in unshakeable. If we're going by this sort of evidence then it's easier to prove rather than disprove the existence of angels.

It's possible that some people *want* angels to exist, as we saw in the story of the Angel of Mons, so that they perhaps view seemingly commonplace experiences in the light of the supernatural. In a way, this is a sort of survival mechanism, since if angels exist then we have to assume that so does a God, and

Robbie Burns • *T.S. Eliot* • *Jeremy Sandford* • *Bruce Chatwin*

therefore an afterlife; ergo, our immortality is assured, in our own minds at least.

The dilemma is that unless we've *had* that direct experience, then for some of us it's hard to suspend disbelief in anything but an empirical world. The problem is further complicated by the fact that many of the encounters that people suppose are angelic are only a little way out of the ordinary, and could often be explained away quite rationally. You know when someone says 'You had to *be* there!'?

One such story — seemingly mundane yet which smacks of angelic intervention — is told by Joan Embury, who lives on the south coast of the UK. Here it is.

The Black Volvo

'About 15 years ago I was running a series of art workshops and was scheduled to do one at a centre in Brighton. The week before the workshops was due I went to recce the space. The weather was absolutely boiling hot.

I'd parked my car in full sun and on the return journey the interior was like a furnace; the age of the car precluded any kind of air-con and even with the windows wide open it was scorching in there. I set off home.

After about five minutes of driving I began to feel very odd — dizzy, light headed, very sick. I knew that these were all the symptoms of heatstroke so I decided to stop at the first available place to park along the seafront as I really didn't feel fit to drive. However, there were cars everywhere, parked up; no space whatsoever to take a break, and by this time I was feeling seriously ill. I was getting worried about how I'd cope with all the traffic that was surrounding me. I was just about aware that I wasn't thinking at all clearly and was relying purely on the

Beryl Nozedar • Trevor Nozedar • Andrew Catlin • Edith Piaf

brake lights of the car ahead of me; when it braked, I braked, and I began to follow it quite blindly. The car in question was an old Volvo, black, very solid and 'safe' looking.

'As we left Hove I remembered that in a mile or two we would pass a big green – if I could make it that far I'd be able to pull in. However, when I got there a JCB was blocking the entrance and again there was nowhere that I could safely pull over. I had to drive on, and became aware that the big old black Volvo was still directly in front of me, travelling in the same direction and at a stately sort of pace that I could cope with. I still felt absolutely dreadful, as though I might black out at any minute, and began to worry about how I would cope when the car would inevitably go its own way – or so I thought. By this time I had reached the outskirts of Worthing and I was sure that the car would carry on along the main road but it didn't; it turned off towards the seafront, which was my route. I began to wonder about this car. When we reached the road where I lived the Volvo actually turned into the road and slowed down by my house as though it was going to park up. But as I pulled up, ready to faint, it turned around and drove off.

'On reflection, later, I felt that this could not possibly be a coincidence. I had so badly needed help on this hellish journey and it came in a form that was practical and reassuring; the solidity of the old car and its gentle pace helped me get home safely'.

For Joan, this experience was certainly not of some apocryphal creature, eyes flashing and wings fluttering; however, help came just when it was needed, and indeed, many of the encounters that people describe as being of the angelic kind follow this pattern; innocuous experiences that *might* be passed off as coincidence but that have some twist about them that elevates from the ordinary and into the realms of the extraordinary. It makes sense that a

Billie Holiday • *James Watt* • *Louis Armstrong* • *The Searys*

helpful angel wouldn't want to give us a heart attack by appearing before us in a guise that's too out of the ordinary.

So, then, how do angels appear to us, if we need to be spared the full-on classic wings-and-halo combo? Let's do a quick roundabout loop into this subject starting with a look at one of the finest latter-day proponents of all things angelic.

Swedenborg

It's worth mentioning Swedenborg here simply because this scholar/scientist/theologian and mystic has had a profound effect on our ideas and thoughts about angels and angelic forms. Born in Stockholm in 1688, it's likely that this son of a bishop would have been heavily influenced by his father's unshakeable belief in the spirit world in general and in both guardian angels and angelic forms in general.

Initially, Swedenborg's interest and expertise in the new sciences and mechanics earned him a great reputation as both scientist and administrator. But the work for which he is remembered today – his theories about and seemingly experiential knowledge of angels – came to him later in life when, at the age of 56, something happened that would inform pretty much all of his work from that moment on. In fact, he started to keep a diary of dreams which provided a powerful catalyst for the ideas that echoed down the centuries to us where they still have relevance today. Indeed, Swedenborg's ideas, like those of Galileo and Da Vinci, were way ahead of his time. For example, he sketched out plans for a flying machine and also a submarine. Whether these ideas were inspired by angelic guidance or not is impossible to say – but bear in mind again that the concept of time isn't as clear-cut as we might imagine it to be.

Swedenborg not only dreamed vividly, but went into trance

states and saw visions in which he claimed direct communication with the angelic realms. It's a mark of his power and credibility, and also an indication of the mood of the times, which was far more overtly open to the idea of celestial powers and heavenly intervention than perhaps it is today, that the King of Sweden patronised him to the extent that he could spend the rest of his life in search of the cosmic and the miraculous.

Swedenborg claimed that God had enabled him to shake off the constraints levied upon 'normal' human beings and that he had the pleasure of instant access to Heaven and Hell and could freely converse with angels and spirits, as well as demons. These new talents evidently included psychic powers, too; there's a famous incident in which Swedenborg told the diners at a party in Gothenburg that there was a fire in Stockholm, some 400km away. This fire, he said, had consumed the home of his neighbour and that his own house was in danger. The dinner continued, and a couple of hours later Swedenborg announced his relief that his house was safe. When news of the fire appeared two days later, Swedenborg's predictions were right on all counts.

Is it possible that Swedenborg was in direct communication with the Powers, who as we have learned are the rulers of all things to do with augury and prophecy?

The central core of Swedenborg's philosophy is that the natural, physical, spiritual and celestial worlds are inextricably linked and that human beings are actually born to become angels. These ideas are outlined in the rather dense 'Heavenly Secrets' or 'Arcana Celestia'. Swedenborg wrote that:

'If our inner part is spiritual, we are actually angels in heaven. This means that we are in a community of angels while we are living in our physical body, even if we are not aware of it. After we are released from our physical bodies, we associate with angels'.

This idea of Swedenborg's, that human beings are born to

Douglas Bader • *Elvis* • *Grace Darling* • *Rosa Parks*

become angels, highlights a point that is raised often and often. Are human beings and angels sometimes the same thing? If, as Swedenborg says, 'we are in a community of angels while we are living in our physical body', is it possible that we are not only a part of those energies, but that they are a part of us? The other idea that equates to Swedenborg's notion is the Dharmic idea that we are reborn onto this plane again and again until we are aware enough, and attuned enough, to achieve spiritual bliss and union with the divine. The truth can be recognised where philosophical ideas coincide.

We encounter lots of stories from the side of the person experiencing angelic energies; we get fewer that show the possibility that there's another side to the story. Here is one such tale.

Dan's Story

Dan is an IT technician in a pharmaceutical company. He lives in Birmingham, in the UK, with his wife and three children.

'A funny thing happened a little while ago that really made me think about the nature of the angelic.

'I needed to be in London for a couple of days for a conference and was very kindly given the keys to a flat belonging to someone I'd never met, a friend of a friend, who was away for a few weeks. The flat was great and I was incredibly grateful to have it, and pleased about the money it was saving me, but I have to say that it was in a pretty rough neighbourhood.

'One evening I was driving home and was just a couple of streets away from the flat when I passed a woman standing on the side of her road by her car. It was about 1am and she looked

Christian Barnard • Simon Clayton • Esti Clayton • Linda and Dominic

distressed; to be honest, I wouldn't have wanted to be a lone female in that part of town.

'I pulled over, aware that I might seem like a threat, too. I wound down the window and asked, as gently as I could, if there was anything wrong. The woman looked hard at me and told me that her bag had been stolen; in it were her car keys, mobile phone, wallet, the lot. I asked her, had she called the police? I was really concerned that she shouldn't be afraid of me.

'She hadn't yet been able to call the police, so I dialled them on my mobile and then handed it to her so she could speak to them, and the AA, and also her family, to tell them what was going on. I stayed in the car so she wouldn't be nervous.

'So far, so good. But then she went all weird and dropped to the ground and started having what seemed to be an epileptic fit. I had never had experience of this before but I knew enough first aid to know I needed to get her into the recovery position, make sure that she was unable to swallow her tongue, and then get an ambulance, which thankfully arrived within the next two minutes.

'I then called the last number she had dialled – her husband – and told him which hospital she was being taken to. I followed the ambulance to make sure she got there, called the AA to tell them what was going on and also called the police for good measure. Job done, I drove home. Except that in all the fuss I lost my own phone somewhere along the way. This meant that even if the woman or her family had wanted to call me, they wouldn't have been able to contact me in any way.

'It occurred to me that I was totally anonymous in this situation, untraceable, and came along just when I was needed, knew what to do, and didn't wait around for thanks – not that this was the reason I helped. Now then, I'm no angel, but if that woman had been me I could very easily understand that she might put my intervention down to angelic forces!'

Marco Polo • *Alex Maiolo* • *Stanley Meyer* • *Nikola Tesla*

Dan's story shows the other side of what is one of the most frequent forms in which we are helped by angels; that of the roadside rescue. We already found out about Bronwen's dramatic roadside rescue in the earlier part of this book. Here's another, which definitely shows the side of the rescued, rather than the rescuer.

Mandy's Story

'I had a fairly stupid idea that I was going to drive across the Atlas mountains just weeks after passing my driving test. I knew nothing about cars and hadn't even driven on a motorway for any great length of time, so the decision to go to a foreign country and drive a strange hire car on the 'wrong' side of the road across fairly remote territory was, looking back on it, a really mad thing to do.

'It's hot during the day but at night the temperature really drops. On my first night I was in two minds as to whether to stay where I was or drive through the night and see the sunrise. I decided to drive through the night and see the sunrise.

'At about 11pm I had a tyre blow-out. I knew the hire car had a spare but I didn't know where it was and I didn't have a clue about how to change it. Even if I had, it was pitch black and I was in the middle of nowhere. The only thing to do was lock the doors of the car and huddle up in the back and wait till the morning.

'It was truly, truly freezing. I was worried about leaving the engine on in case I ran out of battery or petrol; I really was clueless. I'm not scared of the dark, but not knowing exactly where I was, was horrible.

'I'd been trying to sleep for about an hour but not having much luck, when a face loomed in at the window and frightened me half to death. It was a man, quite young-looking, tapping on

Lynne Lauren • Tylluan Penry • Bill Gates • Warren Buffett

the window. I had to shove the key in the ignition to open the window, took quite a while to do it in my befuddled state.

'The stranger asked if he could help, and I explained the situation after I got out of the car. He gave me his woollen jacket to wear and then set to changing the tyre. The weird thing was that under the woollen jacket he was in shirt sleeves and shorts, of all things. He was tall, very good looking, and I'm not sure what nationality. He sounded American, but with the sort of accent that people have when they learn American English from the radio. He could have been European, but I'm really not sure.

'Anyway, he got the tyre on the car and put the old one under the cover in the back seat. The engine started first time. I asked him if he wanted a lift anywhere, but he said no, he was OK. I offered him money for his time, but he just laughed and said to put something in a charity box if I wanted to.

'So I gave him back the cardigan, and set off. It was two or three hours before the peculiarity of the situation really began to dawn on me. I had been in the middle of nowhere. I had been helped by a stranger, foreign to Morocco, who was seemingly walking along in this nowhere in shorts and a shirt and a fairly thin woollen cardigan in temperatures that were just on zero. It was in the middle of the night. He didn't want a lift. He wouldn't take money. What kind of person would be out there like that?

'The next day, I retraced my journey to see where I had been. The only way I could do this was by timing the return journey. There was NOTHING, no signs of civilisation, anywhere close to where I'd been. Do you think that this person might have been some sort of angel?'

This last question is easy to answer; whether or not this person was an angel, he showed distinct evidence of angelic energies.

Prof Alan Jones • *Phillip Carr-Gomm* • *Stephanie Carr-Gomm*

We have to ask ourselves again; are they one and the same? Here's another in the same vein, this time from Janita Hahn, singer with legendary band Babe Ruth;

'A few years, back, I was having a terrible, terrible time. I was in Mid Wales with my friend Tina, it was raining hard, the roads were sheets of mud; it was dark and I'd realised a little while earlier that I was miscarrying my third child, so needed to get home or to a hospital as soon as possible.

'Well, the car stalled in the middle of a huge mud slick that had slid down from the fields at the side of the road. By now it was raining very very hard and we just couldn't get the car to start. I was sobbing; there was no way I could get out and push, and Tina is a tiny girl.

'A man came literally out of nowhere and pushed the car to the side of the road where at least it would be safe from any oncoming traffic. He then proceeded to hitch us to his own car with a rope and towed us all the way home. Then he just sort of disappeared into the night. That was definitely the action of an angel; whether it was a 'real' angel or a human being acting like one sort of doesn't really matter'.

Yuri Gagarin • *Buddy Holly* • *Ennio Morricone*

10
Madman or Visionary?

So, it seems that sometimes people see angels without the intervention of any external agent; sometimes there's an outside factor involved, whether that be chemically-induced, triggered by meditation, or whatever. We need to make a distinction between a vision and a hallucination, between the madman who is derided for the things that he sees, and the visionary who is lauded for the same reasons.

Although we can have 'bad' visions, in general they are accepted as positive and uplifting, possibly life-changing, experiences. A vision can alter the course of someone's life as they realise that there's more to things than meets the eye – a reminder of those unseen aspects of the universe which angelic energies, amongst other phenomena, are a part of.

People talk about having visions of God, angels, light. Sometimes we have visions of departed loved ones, who might give us information or just simply appear to us. Whether these apparitions are genuine or whether they are the product of imagination is a debate that will no doubt rage for some time to come, but there's no doubt that such visions can be very

David Lynch · Amy Johnson · Donald Campbell · Amelia Earhart

reassuring, especially when they happen to a grieving person. There are numerous instances of someone having a vision of a person and later finding that the person died at around the same time as the experience. The regularity with which this phenomenon occurs makes it logical to suppose that this might be some way of saying goodbye. Conversely, dying people sometimes have visions of friends and relatives who have died, as though they are coming to help them go over to the 'other side'. Such visions are common throughout the entire world, not restricted to any single culture or religious belief.

It seems that there's a thin line between what is considered sane and what is not in people who have visions. For example, the great artist and writer William Blake is often described as a 'visionary' and it's true that a great deal of what inspired him came from realms that are not easily accessible to normal human beings. We define someone as 'mad' only when their behaviour runs contrary to the common precepts of society; a 'visionary' is relatively fine so long as he or she doesn't do anything to upset the balance of that society too much. Blake described his visions thus:

'A vision is not a cloudy vapour or a "nothing". It is organized and minutely articulated beyond all that the mortal and perishing nature can produce. I assert that all my visions appear to me infinitely more perfect and more organised than anything seen by the mortal eye.'

Some of us are subject to visions as a result of a mental instability, such as schizophrenia. The problem comes when we try to discern what a 'real' vision is, and what is not. I would argue that, to the visionary, no matter how it happens, one vision is as valid as any other. Some schizophrenics have visions that are neither uplifting nor pleasant; demons, bogey men and all sorts of nasties can lurk in the innermost depths of our

John Morris • Ron Edwards • David Lynch • Henry Miller

subconscious minds. Gaining 'control' of these internal monsters is vitally important for the well-being of the person that experiences them and sometimes, as we'll see in an anecdote later, it's important that the 'good' visions remain whilst the 'bad' ones stay in a manageable place. Of course, visions are not always 'seen'; sometimes they are auditory. They can take the form of disembodied voices, singing, music.

Now we come on to hallucinations. Again, broadly speaking, these differ from visions in that they can be the result of external factors – drugs, for example. We can also have what seem to be hallucinations when we are extraordinarily tired. A good example, and one that I guess most of us have experienced, is the mistake of thinking that a roadside post or pillar is a person when we're driving late at night in a state of extreme exhaustion. Strictly speaking, this isn't a hallucination but an illusion; our tired mind is playing tricks on us. Hallucinations can be dangerous in that they can be so convincing that they can 'control' the person, who might be convinced that the phenomenon that he or she is experiencing is actually real. A good example is the delusion of being able to fly that sometimes happens under the influence of certain types of drugs. This can be so utterly convincing – the logical mind completely overridden by faulty chemical messages – that people have injured themselves very badly and even died.

So, how do we differentiate between the sorts of visions encountered by Blake and other mystics, and the delusions and hallucinations experienced by less fortunate individuals? What tells us that the encounters with angels and demons that we read about in the Bible are somehow different to the ravings of a lunatic? A give-away factor that the visions might be 'real' is that the person might be reluctant to talk about it; he or she is aware of the boundaries common to society and does not wish to be

Doug and Joy • *Ellen Macarthur* • *Jont* • *Oppenheimer*

derided as 'insane'. We are all a part of society and hopefully we have an inherent understanding of what is acceptable and what is not. It's funny, because part of my reasoning for wanting to write this book in the first place was to try to make talking about such matters more acceptable than they currently are, to allow people to 'come out' about some of their experiences without being afraid of being seen as insane. It's only by talking about these things that we're able to understand them.

There are numerous examples of historical figures whose visions have become renowned. Many of the saints of the early Catholic Church are numbered amongst these luminaries. Hildegard of Bingen's visions were incredibly numerous and vivid, but she resisted talking about them until one of the people who populated her extraordinary visions actually explained to her that she needed to tell people about what she was seeing and hearing; this was part of her destiny and indeed, it's why she is still so famous. Similarly, St Theresa of Avila, now renowned for the ecstasies that she experienced, had no-one that she could confide in and was concerned that people would call her insane. Although she was subsequently canonised, Theresa felt that what was happening to her was very definitely her own personal experience and that there was no reason for her to be lauded in the way she was; the visions happened despite her, not because of her. Here's what she said about it:

'I repeat it; you feel and see yourself carried away you know not whither. For though we feel how delicious it is, yet the weakness of our nature makes us afraid at first...so trying is it that I would very often resist and exert all my strength, particularly at those times when the rapture was coming on me in public'.

Theresa's experiences include eyewitness accounts of her physically rising into the air; on one occasion, when she felt the

Freud • Jung • You • Picasso • Lyn and Margaret Regan

'rapture' starting to happen to her, some of the other nuns around her tried to hold her down but were unable to prevent her floating upwards. Unsurprisingly, St Theresa prayed that she would be spared these extraordinary attentions, but despite this, it seems that they persisted. Do people still have these sorts of extreme experiences? Did St Theresa really float up into the air, a feat which was witnessed by many? We'll never know for sure, but it's worth bearing in mind that the context of her vocation rendered these supernatural events acceptable. If a lay person had started to float up into the air – particularly if that person happened to be a woman – it's more than likely that demonic forces, rather than celestial ones, would have been blamed.

In essence, for the true visionary, the visions that they experience seem to help them to make better sense of the world, to integrate with the universe rather than be isolated from it. We also need to bear in mind that the standards by which we define 'normality' change frequently, and it could well be, that had St Theresa been living in these times, she might well be undergoing treatment for schizophrenia.

These days, we can treat such imbalances to a certain extent, but I was lucky enough to be given a very frank and moving story from someone who has suffered from schizophrenia and has managed to reconcile the good parts of the experience whilst being able to accept the bad parts for what they are.

Tom's Story

'I don't really want to go into massive details about the diagnosis of my condition or the colossally upsetting effect it has had on certain aspects of my life. After a long struggle, I now feel fully reconciled to my state of being, so much so that I can see advantages in some of the things that I see and hear. There

Me • Ptolemy • JK Rowling • JRR Tolkien

may be voices sometimes in my head that tell me that I'm useless and rubbish, but I know how to ignore them, and after all, doesn't everyone have this sort of thing going on in their lives from time to time? I have something extra which many people don't have. I can see and hear a particular being, who I call an angel. She is a very beautiful but very old woman, who whispers encouraging things in my ear, and always seems to be there when I am down. I don't call for her; she just comes. I don't tell many people about her because I know exactly what they'll think, because of my diagnosed medical condition. They would think that this lovely thing is all part of the madness. Whether it is or not doesn't really matter. But to me, this person is real, is positive, and enhances my life'.

Tom is a diagnosed paranoid schizophrenic who has struggled to gain mastery over the things that he sees and the voices that he hears. He's now aware – although this wasn't always the case – that there are certain things that he experiences which are outside of the remit of 'normal' society, and he now knows how to temper them to fit in with what is acceptable within these boundaries. He's able to separate the good from the bad and indeed sees his visions as an extra skill, a sort of superpower, if you like.

In terms of the 'truth' of the accounts of angelic sightings and interventions that I have had during the course of researching this book, it's noticeable that the stories which feel to be the most truthful are those which have required some coaxing – like Tom's.

Pablo Casals • *Jaqueline DuPrey* • *Maria Callas* • *Carl Sagan*

11

Angels of Birth

It's noticeable that Angels often appear at times of greatest stress. One of the most frightening and stressful times a woman could ever experience must be when giving birth. Will everything be OK? Will the baby be healthy? Will the medical services be up to scratch? What could go wrong?

I feel very fortunate in having been given this next account and I repeat it here verbatim. It comes from one of my favourite authors, Judika Illes, whose books on all things magickal are the best you can buy. Here's Judika's account of what happened when she had her first baby.

'I saw an angel once. In the delivery room right after I had given birth.

'I had an earlier miscarriage and a protracted period of infertility and so, although I really liked being pregnant, felt very good and actually had very easy pregnancies, it was a very stressful time, if only because I was aware of how much could go wrong. Long story short, the hospital made me nervous, the physician made me nervous (I had wanted a home birth but my husband at that time absolutely refused.) Although everything

Jonathan Cainer • Dame Margot Fonteyn • Nureyev • The Heathies Ghandi

was fine, there were issues with the birth (conceptual differences between myself and physicians/hospital). I had various profound spiritual experiences just prior and during this pregnancy and I carried a lot of fear.

'Immediately after giving birth, I became aware of the presence of an angel. I did not see him appear: one second he wasn't there, and then he was. I knew I was the only one in the room (doctor, nurse, husband there too) who was aware of the angel but that didn't surprise me because I've seen ghosts all my life and am used to seeing things that others don't.

'The angel was a glowing being of incredibly intense light and radiated heat, although not proportionate to the intensity of the light. I could not keep my eyes open in his presence. He was blinding. In school, as a kid, I once saw a film on the bombs dropped on Hiroshima and Nagasaki. A survivor explained that the light of the atomic flash was so blinding that you could see even with your eyes shut tight, right through your lids. This was the same. Even with my eyes shut, I could see the angel. He was a large, tall, silent, winged, golden being. Unspeakably beautiful. I cannot overemphasize the intensity of light radiated.

'The first thought that came unbidden to my mind was "Raphael is here. Everything is alright". And I felt safe and protected and knew that everything would be fine. (And it was.) The angel did not communicate with me or even look at me. It was at the foot of my bed and there for the baby, not for me but I immediately relaxed.

'Next thoughts: I was cognisant that what I was seeing corresponded exactly to biblical and Cabalistic descriptions of angels. I was then sure that these were actually written down by people actually describing their own experiences – not just made up. I don't think I saw what I expected to see, if only because this wasn't something I expected to see but when I saw what I did, I recognized the similarity. As if you had never seen a tiger before but someone described one to you and then you saw one and knew it was what had been described.

'Also I felt very humbled – because I hadn't asked for that experience or worked for it. I am aware (was aware at that moment) that there are people who spend lifetimes attempting to induce just such an experience – who go through tremendous effort, expense, time, ritual in order to receive such an apparition and yet I had received it without asking and without any effort. There the angel was. Eventually he (and I have always felt confident that it was Raphael, that somehow I recognized him or that he transmitted that information although I have no proof of this nor did he verbally identify himself) wasn't there. But the glow that I felt lingered for a very long time. And in my mind's eye, I can still see what I saw then'.

As if this story wasn't enough, I received a further account which has great similarities, the most notable being the name of the angelic being who another first-time mother encountered during a time of extraordinary fear. This comes from Helen, who lives on the south coast of the UK.

'I haven't told this story to very many people. Let's say that the work that I do has to be very clear, concise and matter-of-fact, and much as I'd love to tell people about this experience, it wouldn't go down well with either my colleagues or clients. So, my telling you this here is my way of contributing to the evidence for angels without me losing my livelihood or people thinking that I'm insane. Also, this was such a precious experience that I don't want to deface it with people's opinions about it, especially if they give it a mundane explanation.

'Some context for you; I had always pooh-poohed the idea of

Tony Benn • *Joanna Lumley* • *Keir Hardie* • *T E Lawrence*

any sorts of spiritual beings; ghosts, fairies, angels, God, the lot, were all consigned to the dustbin of my mind. I have a very pragmatic approach to life — or at least, I used to. Since this event I have changed my mind about many things and I can see that there might be career changes in the future because of it.

'I was heavily pregnant with my first child. I knew exactly when he was going to be born, knew his name (or at least, I thought I did), had my case packed, everything organised. Typical me. The baby had other ideas, though, everything kicked off unexpectedly and I was rushed into hospital for an emergency C-section a week early. I won't go into detail, but suffice to say that all my being was screaming out, silently, with fear as I was racing along in the ambulance, sirens blaring. I had never experienced real terror in my life but now I know what it feels like. The sheer panic of the emergency services was enough for me to know that this was very, very serious, and I knew that the life of my unborn child was in the balance.

'Then something miraculous happened. I felt a definite presence, behind me, around me, warm, soothing, embracing, loving; I found that all the fear lifted away as though it had been a heavy blanket, and I felt my being suffused with something light and — the only word I can describe it as — a kind of gracefulness. I felt as though I were in a state of grace. I heard in my mind some words, "all will be well", and also I heard the name "Raphael". Apparently there were tears streaming down my cheeks but I can't remember anything else except for that transported, elevated feeling, and the feeling of being lifted, suffused with light.

'All *was* well; my baby was fine. He's a healthy five-year-old now, and his name is Raphael. He's called Raff for short but I wouldn't say he's always particularly angelic right now!'

I'm very grateful for these two stories. They are about an

Richard Burton • *Finlay, Janette and Tyler* • *George Harrison*

intimate and profound experiences at the most special and sacred time that any woman will ever encounter. Next, let's look at some stories of the angelic beings that seem to guide us through other crucial stages in our lives. Let's see what angels are there to help us when we die.

Terry Gilliam • *David Lean* • *Michelangelo* • *Jim Morrison*

12

Angels of Death

The Angel of Death has become an object of fear, and something to be avoided. However, if there's one universal truth that brings us all together, rich and poor, it is that we will certainly experience the thing that we call death, perhaps according to some philosophies, many times over. It stands to reason, then, that although we might fear the Angel of Death there really is no need to.

Some societies believe that certain animals are psychopomps – that is, that they guide us from this world to the next one. These animals include dogs, horses, and in some parts of India, cows. It's a comforting thought that there may be angelic beings and energies that can help us on this most interesting of journeys.

John's Story

John is an electrician, living in Germany, with his wife and two small children. He's a very bluff, pragmatic sort of a chap, not one given to fanciful ideas and not necessarily the sort of person that I had expected to respond to my requests for stories.

Frank Capra • Yoav • Kelly Joe Phelps • Otis Redding

'The first part of this story isn't mine, really, but my Granddad's. He'd fought as a young man in the First World War and was sent to France. He saw some pretty horrendous things and had been lucky to survive, from what I could make out. As a kid I'd ask about stuff constantly. He'd just give me titbits then, but when I got older and my interest was less gratuitous, he expanded and told me more.

'One particular time, he was part of a battle in which a lot of his friends were killed. He told me that, as he watched from a vantage point he'd managed to get to, he watched balls of light hover over some of the bodies... the bodies also sort of emanated the same sort of ball of light, the two lights melded together and floated off upwards.

'My granddad reckoned that these were the souls of the dying men, being met by their guardian angels and taken up to Heaven. I'm not religious, but that seems to make sense to me.

'My granddad lived to be a ripe old age and used to say he wasn't afraid of dying, because he'd been a witness to the process'.

There are strong parallels between this story and that of Vickie, a nurse who works in a hospice. The similarity exists not only in the light that they both saw leaving the dying bodies, but the meeting and melding with a similar body of light which then float upwards as one entity.

Vickie's Story

Vickie is a plump, jolly woman aged about 50. She has an infectious laugh – and she laughs a lot. She's a very nice person to spend time with. Vickie works in a hospice in the south of England.

The Buddha • *Otis Redding* • *Neil Young* • *Jeff Beck*

'I'd never really given much thought to angels, to be honest. I was working for a few years as an agency nurse and was too busy just getting on with the job to get into anything too metaphysical!

'Then a few years back I decided to change tack a bit, and went to work in a hospice. With two young children, a permanent place of work made life much easier.

'It was after a few months in the hospice that I started seeing what you might call angels. I can't think of any other way to describe them.

'The first time was when I was working on a night shift. I was reading a book and keeping an eye on things, when I suddenly felt compelled to go to check on a lady – I'll call her Beatrice but that's not her real name.

'Beatrice was sleeping peacefully, but there was a distinct 'presence' at the end of her bed. It was like a tall tower of pale light; not a ghost, not at all like a ghost. I've seen those too, by the way! And it didn't seem in any way unusual.

'I went back to my desk and it was only an hour or so later, after I'd done a few little jobs and was having a cup of tea, that I started to think about what I'd seen and it dawned on me that this being or presence was out of the ordinary. It actually made me laugh to think how 'normal' it had seemed.

'After that first time, I became more accustomed to seeing these beings, generally at the ends of people's beds. It was almost as though, having seen that first one, I was somehow tuned in to them. I also started to notice that the people in question always died very soon after, and it's now got to the point that I can alert other staff and sometimes I can even let the family know, in a fairly roundabout way, that they might like to look in on such and such a day.

'Then, I witnessed someone at the moment of their death. The being had been present at the end of the bed, but this time

Carlos Castenada • *David Attenborough* • *Brian Eno* • *Peter Gabriel*

I saw the same sort of light emanating from the person as his soul let go of his body. The being and the spirit joined up, sort of waited or hovered for a while, and then just floated upwards.

'It was a beautiful thing, really, really beautiful. I've seen this several times, now, and every time it happens I'm filled with a great sense of wonder.

'I feel really privileged to do the job that I do. I can tell people for sure that death is not the end, because of what I can see. I'm now training to be a grief counsellor, but I'm aware that not everyone will be receptive to the information that I have. I have to be a bit careful sometimes about it.

'I know for an absolute fact that I am not the only person in the hospital to have such experiences. I have spoken about it with other members of staff, but for the most part it's not discussed openly, just accepted as part of living and dying, an everyday part of working in a hospice.

'Does the thought of death worry me or frighten me in any way? Not in the least!'

The next story isn't from a hospital, but bears a remarkable similarity to the stories that precede it, again, in the orbs of light seen by the witness.

Dave's Story

'I'm a long distance lorry driver working in the UK, doing deliveries from one end of the country to another. Six months ago I was en route as usual when I get stuck in a jam – I was fairly close to the front of the queue, caused by an overturned car. There's nothing to do in a situation like that but turn the engine off and wait. So I was just sitting there, not really thinking about anything, mind switched off.

Bob Geldof • Bono • John Martyn • Chrissie Hynde

'I was looking towards where the accident (I couldn't actually see what had happened, there were other vehicles ahead of me) must have been when I saw a golden-ish ball of light coming down from somewhere. As I watched, I saw another, smaller ball of light float up to meet it then they sort of merged together and drifted off, gradually fading into the sky not very high up.

'I sat there a bit puzzled. It's funny how you try to rationalise things. I said to myself maybe it was a trick of the light but I knew it was something else really. It was on the news later that one poor person had died in this crash and I wonder if the light I saw was the soul of the person being collected by a guardian of some kind; I'm a bit reluctant to say the "A" word because I am a lorry driver after all!'

Dave actually told his girlfriend about his experience, and it was her promptings that made him get in touch.

The following story is from Veronica:
'I was blessed to have seen a 'host' of angels just two hours before the death of my mother in-law back in September 2007.

'My mother in-law, Joan, was a lovely lady who was adored not only by her family but by just about anybody who met her. People use the term "heart of gold" and although I have met many wonderful people, Joan was the true definition of the phrase. She really did have a heart of gold and had a fabulous sense of humour, too. She was taken into hospital with a heart problem and had a very short, shocking illness before she passed away.

'I went to see Joan on the morning of her death. She was heavily sedated and I was very upset to see her like this. At 6.10pm my husband and my two daughters were sitting having their tea in the kitchen. I just wasn't hungry so I sat in the conservatory just a few feet away.

Brancusi • George Best • Pele • Django Reinhardt • Sherpa Tensing

'There was a clear blue sky that evening. I looked to my right and couldn't believe what I was seeing. I saw a formation of angels in the clouds so perfectly clear they couldn't have been painted any more clearly. The angels numbered six or seven (this is the only thing I'm not certain of) at approximately a 30 degree angle to where I was sitting. They had beautifully-shaped wings. Behind this group of angels was a single angel that was as big as all the angels in front and behind this very large one I saw a cherub. I looked away a number of times, blinking, since I could not quite believe what I was seeing. The angels hardly seemed to move at all. I kept looking, aghast, at what I was witnessing.

'I then called my daughter who I knew had read about angels and she told me, "I asked the angels to help Nan".

'Strangely, I had absolutely no inclination to call my husband to look and didn't even think to grab my camera. This blissful event was to become even more astounding because as I continued to watch this amazing sight I then became aware of my mind becoming totally calm and cleared, and then into my head came these words: "We have come to gather her".

'I am emotional just thinking of this moment as it was so poignant and special. Joan passed away two hours after this event.

'I now believe this message was meant for me, because under normal circumstances I would have asked everyone else to look at these angels, and yet I didn't even think of doing such a thing. I also think that someone was 'looking out for me'. I had been through quite a stressful time prior to this event. My father had died the previous Christmas Eve after a long battle with cancer and clinical depression, at the same time my daughter was ill with M.E. and my husband had a serious eye condition. A while before my father's death I had started my own quest to become emotionally and spiritually stronger. I had studied Reiki healing and was an avid reader of spiritual and self healing books (and

Alexandra David-Neal • Miles Davis • David Tomlinson

still am!). I feel that all I have learned has helped me to get through these tough times.

'I don't shout from the roof tops about my angel encounter but I am happy to tell anyone who is interested. It was an encounter that I will never ever forget, and I feel so blessed for having had this experience'.

David McAlmont • Glenn Miller • Danny Kaye • Chi Fi Masters

13

Children as Angels?

There's a relatively common belief that those of us who die very young are 'taken away' to become angels. Now, you could argue that this is a response to the incredible grief that any parent must feel at the death of a child, and could be sort of coping mechanism. What matters for the parent is that this idea is a comfort and may enable them to make sense of such a devastating loss. Some stories, however, send a shiver up the spine and have a ring of 'truth' about them; here is one such story.

Anna's Story

Anna is a tall, elegant lady originally from the USA. She's incredibly vibrant and alive; energy fizzes and crackles from every pore, and she looks way younger than her 50+ years. She is purposeful, driven and confident and has the appearance of a great inner strength and tranquillity. However, Anna is the first to tell you that she wasn't always this way:

'For years, I was incredibly miserable because I couldn't have a child. We tried various methods for about 12 years and the

Gustave Klimt • *Gustave Holst* • *Vaughan Williams* • *Stravinsky*

whole process was making me ill and my husband depressed. As well as being a physically strenuous process, it's mental torture for both partners especially when you fail to conceive month after month, year after year. Our marriage was pretty much on the rocks when IVF worked; we'd decided that this was to be the very last time and it was like a miracle. I could hardly dare to believe that I was actually pregnant.

'The pregnancy itself was horrible. I'd expected a glorious and joyous experience but it was truly awful.

'When Serena was born, the nine months of hell were wiped out and I was so happy; unfortunately I was so wrapped up in my little girl that eventually the death knell sounded for my marriage, although my husband was and is a wonderful, generous and patient person and we remain friends. However, it had taken a long time before Serena came into my life and she absorbed every minute. There is no doubt that I drove him away, transferring absolutely all of my affections to my beautiful daughter.

'One night I had a very vivid dream. Serena was in a school play, dressed up in the sort of typical angel outfit that little girls wear in Nativity plays; white smock dress, a tinsel halo and cardboard tin foil wings, and in particular I remembered her bare feet since even in the dream I was worried that she might catch a cold!

'In the dream, Serena came to the front of the stage and addressed me directly (I was in the audience like any proud parent).

'She said; "Mummy, I have to go away from you now for a while. I have to go back to be a proper angel, because I have to help you with something quite big, and I'm only a little girl".

'Then other weird stuff happened, like it does in dreams. I didn't think too hard about it but luckily I did write the dream down; anything to do with Serena formed the absolute pivotal

Beethoven • *Heinrich Biber* • *Rudolf Steiner* • *Paganini*

point of my life. I just assumed that the dream came from my own anxiety.

'Three weeks later, Serena died. It was very, very sudden and there was nothing that anyone could have done. It seems that she had a heart defect and was unlikely to have lived very long. It made the fact that she had been born in the first place even more of a miracle.

'My life fell completely, utterly apart. I was devastated beyond reason; I felt as though I was in a black hole, a wind tunnel of empty nothingness; I thought I understood the meaning of the word despair but until this happened, I had had no idea. Suicide crossed my mind more than once.

'When I was at my absolute lowest ebb, strung out on various pills and had finally decided to end it all, I dreamed about Serena once more.

'This dream was incredibly clear; I think they call it "lucid". In the dream Serena was again dressed as the angel, except that the halo and the wings were real and very, very bright. At first I could hardly look at her. She was still Serena, but different. And again she spoke directly to me: "Anna, it's time for you to stop being sad. I told you I was going away for a while, but I'm always with you and I'm going to help you. Please stop being sad".

'It didn't seem odd that she addressed me as "Anna" rather than "Mummy".

'I'm aware that this might sound fanciful, but when I awoke it was as though a veil had been lifted from my eyes. I felt like a completely different person and I had the profound realisation that there is no such thing as death. I wasn't sure what I should do next, but I gave up the pills, galvanised myself, started going out and meeting friends, went horse riding which I hadn't done since I was a child; I started to enjoy my life again, and to be grateful for it. Then, a friend offered me a ticket to go with her

Carlos Santana • *W B Yeats* • *William Blake* • *Ted Hughes*

to Nepal – another friend had pulled out. To cut a long story short, I ended up funding the building of a school for orphans, and it is this work which I know to be my 'mission'; it's this work that I know Serena had to leave me to help with, and I see her in the faces of the children we look after.

'I'll say again that the most profound part of this experience is the knowledge that there really is no such thing as death. For me, this is beyond any belief or faith in a God. It feels like the best-kept secret, which I am privileged to be party to'.

Of the many moving stories in this book, it's this one that actually made me weep. I can't imagine anything worse than losing a child, but the resolution of this tragic event is positive, uplifting and joyous. I'm very grateful to Anna for sharing this with us.

Virginia Woolf • *Mo Mowlam Einstein* • *Debussy* • *Mozart*

14

Sex Angels

I'd say it's odds on that not many books about angels take into account the important part that sex has to play in accessing and experiencing angelic energies – and demonic ones, too, for that matter. Of course, there's an underlying perception that angels are the province of the pious, and that sex has nothing to do with either. This is wrong, and I'll try to explain why.

In the West, specifically, it's a pity that the influence of certain aspects of the predominant faith groups has frequently, and sadly, rendered the beauty of the sexual experience into one of shame and guilt. Sex outside of marriage, gay sex, sex for the purposes of pleasure rather than procreation; in certain sectors, all these physical pleasures are frowned upon. And yet the power of the sensual, sexual experience, it seems, can offer a conduit to angelic communication. In the words of the Rev Dr Joseph Fletcher of the Episcopal Theological School: 'The Christian Churches must shoulder much of the blame for the confusion, ignorance, and guilt which surrounds sex in Western culture...The Christian Church, from its earliest primitive beginnings, had been swayed by many Puritanical people, both Catholic and Protestant, who have viewed sex as inherently evil'.

Capability Brown • Frank Lloyd Wright • Norman Foster

This all started with Adam's supposed 'corruption' by Eve in the Garden of Eden, when she disobeyed the commands of God in order to share with Adam the 'fruit of knowledge'. The Church teaches that Jesus Christ died at the cross without ever having had the pleasure of a sexual relationship, and one person who some suspect might have been a partner of his, Mary Magdalene, has been vilified as a prostitute, and much of her story removed from the conventional versions of the Gospels.

Despite this, it's probably true to say that the first truly startling experience that we experience is that of orgasm. Can you remember the first time it happened to you? We might have read about it or be fully conversant with the mental and physical processes that take place when one happens, but no theory can prepare us for the surprise — and shock — of the actual physical experience, especially the first time that it happens.

And yet we tend to categorise such a profoundly important part of our lives as saucy, or titillating, or something to be kept under cover. At the risk of sounding controversial, I'd have to point out that the obsession with pornographic imagery that's prevalent today is a sign of an unhealthy repression if ever one were needed.

Yet again, for an idea of the true profundity of the sexual experience and its place in spirituality, we have to look to the East. For example, the erotic temple carvings and statuary that we find in Asia, including the Kama Sutra and the Yab Yum symbol (male and female entwined in a physical personification of the yin-yang) all point towards the celebration of the transformative and transcendent powers of sex, and the possibility that the physical body can connect with the spiritual realms.

The beauty of sex as a transformative power wasn't always repressed in the West. Nor is it still the case amongst latter-day 'pagan' circles. The faiths that existed before the early Church, and which worshipped the Great Goddess and the Great Mother, made sex the central focus of their worship. The Mystery Cults of Ancient Greece followed the same principles. This very honest, truthful and powerful way of acknowledging and worshipping the Divine within us was subsequently replaced by the Holy Sacrament, which combines matter and spirit, male and female, in a symbolic way, rather than in a practical one. Sadly, the Christian Church condemned the Sacred Goddess and took away the former reverence for the term 'harlot', rendering it into something disgusting, lewd and evil, rather than sacred and beautiful.

The Harlot Priestess

There is a theory that the word 'harlot' has its origins in a Hebrew word meaning 'Priestess'. Hesiod said that these women 'mellowed the behaviour of men' with their sexual magic. These women, personifications of the Goddess, were not only the dispensers of transformational experiences via sexual congress, but were respected also as prophetesses, seers, and sorceresses. They were also renowned as healers, their spittle, for example, believed to cure blindness.

The priestesses who also danced became known as Hours, or Houris. To communicate sexually with the Harlot Priestess was considered to be an initiatory rite for a man, enabling him to become spiritually enlightened. This process is possibly interpreted in the Bible as being given 'visions'.

The importance of the harlot-whore, and the power that it gave to women, was so important that it posed a significant threat to the early Christian Church, and so the profession was vilified. The sexual act was not obliterated, but the whore was defined as a lascivious, licentious woman liable to deter the man

Josh Homme • *Kurt Cobain* • *David Bowie* • *Frank Sinatra*

from his true spiritual path and ultimate salvation rather than lead him to it, as had previously been the case.

So, you might be asking, what has all this to do with visions of, or encounters with, angels?

We need to go back again to the transcendent powers of orgasm, the electrifying cosmic embrace that truly can 'make the earth move' at least, in metaphysical terms!

Tantric practice has been popularised of late; we read of certain rock stars who are apparently able to 'go at it' for days, keeping the actual moment of crisis at bay until the crucial moment. But tantric practices are not simply about raising sexual energy to a crescendo level. This energy – the same source as that of all creativity – is symbolised by the coiled female serpent called Kundalini which lies curled at the base of the spine. This energy is considered to be sacred, holy, and divine. Both historical and contemporary accounts of Kundalini awakenings tell similar stories; they describe that altered states and unusual perceptions engendered by the spontaneous transcendent sexual experiences that are the result of the release of this sacred energy. Images of sages in whom the Kundalini has been awakened often show light pouring down from the crown chakra; this is so close to the haloes of enveloping light that we see in Church iconography that we can assume its one and the same thing as celestial or angelic energies.

The Snake Lady of this Kundalini, when fully activated, courses through two channels, the male and female circuitry in the human body. In sexual congress, these energies fuse between the partners, effectively linking the pair with the energy, or soul, of the universe.

Sometimes this happens spontaneously; sometimes, people practise for many years to attain such a state of union and bliss. During the course of my research I have found some people who equate the energy produced during lovemaking with angelic energies, and a few for whom tantric practises open a sort of door through which such energies can enter, sometimes as a tangible feeling, sometimes as a visible being, sometimes as an unseen but present 'third' that is produced by far more that the sum of two physical parts.

Interestingly, the idea of a hermaphroditic being is a symbol that recurs throughout many religions, a perfect union between male and female energies. The idea of a God or Goddess is really just our human way of needing to categorise everything; the notion of a Great Spirit that is of neither sex but which encompasses both is more acceptable. These 'beings of light' exist not only independently as avatars or as angels, but this same glow appears in the countenances of biblical and other religious figures – such as the Buddha – after an encounter with such energies. We've already mentioned the raptures of such historical personages such as Theresa of Avila, who was actually canonised for what sounds very like extreme 'turns' of erotic, sexually-charged energy.

Let's have a look at some latter-day examples of when the link between sexual and angelic energies has become apparent.

Roxanne's Story*

'I am a sex therapist, working in New York. I got into this line of work because I used to be what they call a sex worker, the person that some people refer to as a prostitute, someone that sells their body for money. I had gotten into this profession because it was the quickest easiest way to get money for drugs. It's not a nice place to be, believe me.

'I've had to face up to a lot of things over the past few years. I

*Assumed name

Bunuel   •   Terry   Gilliam   •   Degas   •   Diaghilev

used to blame what had happened to me on other people, and I used to say I was a good girl till whatever happened, but that wasn't right. I'd always been not exactly bad, but the kid in school that always got told off for being insolent and disrespectful. I couldn't wait to grow up. I was adopted by my grandma because my father wasn't around and my mother wasn't really capable for various reasons, but while I used to use this as an excuse for how I was, now I know that other people have equal shitty stuff in their backgrounds and they don't do what I did.

'I first had sex when I was 12. You'll see that I say "had sex" and not "made love". I loved having sex with different boys because I think it made me feel wanted; like I say, this is not an excuse, just the truth.

'My grandma was lovely to me but I was horrid to her and I couldn't wait to get away and into New York. I left when I was 15. I know I caused her a lot of pain.

'I dabbled with soft drugs like all kids do nowadays, some even younger than me, and by the time I was 16 I was into just about everything; you name it, I'd smoke it, swallow it, snort it. It was when I got the taste for crack that I started turning tricks and sleeping with guys for money and it was then that things really started to go from bad to worse; I was strung out all the time just trying to make enough for the next hit.

'I was living in a shared house with some other girls and we used to take turns with the bedrooms. One day a guy came asking for me. I was about 24 by this time and if I'm honest I'm lucky to have survived. Anyway, this guy I've never heard of is shown to where I am. I've never seen him before and I ask him how he knows me but he just laughs and says he's always known me. I'm like, whatever. He's a beautiful guy, strong-looking, athletic, he has great hair and most of all I remember his smell. Clean, fresh, like the air in a green place with lots of trees.

Leonardo Da Vinci • *Oscar Van Gelden* • *Chris Heywood* • *Galileo*

'It was with him that I realised the difference between having sex and making love. He really made love to me, like I was a real person and not just a hole. It lasted for ages and for the first time in my entire life I had an orgasm; I'd read about them and thought I might have had one, but there was no mistaking this feeling; I wanted it to go on, and on, and it sort of did, for some while. As it was happening, the room filled with light, and he became an angel; I could see the wings, the glow around him as we were together. I heard music and a ringing in my head.

'I know that people will think, oh, she was just a druggy girl experiencing orgasm for the first time, that's all, no angels involved'

'But after he left I laid and wept, for everything I'd done, all the things I hadn't done, all the people I'd lied to or stolen from, all the filthy places I'd put myself. I felt clean, fresh, a new person, like I'd had a spiritual detox. I think for the first time in my life I understood everything completely, I understood what love really was.

'I hadn't asked for any money from this guy. But the next day an envelope arrived with a thousand dollars cash, a bus ticket back to my grandma's small town and the name of a clinic where I could get help. There wasn't a note but I knew who it was from. But the weird thing is, I hadn't told him where my grandma was or anything about her, or about me, for that matter.

'Because of my experience, I know just how great and lovely sex is, and after I cleaned myself up I decided that I'd show people what this angel had shown me. Good sex in a loving, caring relationship can make people whole again. After all we're material beings, right, and this is something that we can do, right?

'Some people say that Jesus never had a girlfriend, never had sex, as if that's something to be proud of. We suppress ourselves for no reason, we deny joy and beauty.

Fra Angelico • *Alexander Graham Bell* • *Stravinsky* • *Magellan*

'My life has changed because of the angel that came to me that day. You can tell me he wasn't an angel if you want, but that's what I want to believe, and this was my experience'.

Next up is a story from one of the three people who had no problem with me revealing his full name in this part of the book. Tiger Koehn is a drummer and producer with cult band The New Creatures. He's also a martial arts expert. Here's his story; I've included his interesting preamble which shows some context and gives an idea of where he's coming from.

Tiger's Story

'All I can really tell you is that any angelic or angel experiences I've had are few, but they've been heavy.

'I know, as I can only assume you do, that the depictions and iconography surrounding what a vast majority of people view as angels had been created by the Catholic Church in and around the Dark Ages. The sublime winged creatures in flowing smocks flapping around in the heavens carrying out edicts of a Supreme Being.

'Between you and me, the five Books of Moses have a very different take on the whole matter, as does the Qur'an and the New Testament. The ancient Indian beliefs are also quite interesting. Since the word itself means 'Messenger' in Hebrew, there are several variations as to the roles that angels are meant to play, or their titles. Another one is Meakh Elohim, which means 'messenger of God'. There are a few more definitions. I really think people today are quite confused as to what they really are. I suppose each person's belief depends on which faith you choose to attach yourself to.

'I find the story of the Kaballah, and the versions of the

angelic wars, the most fascinating. There are many, many different categories of angels, both good and evil. Is all this an incredible true history, or a fabulous myth? Who is to say?

'I have to tell you, my personal experiences come in, well, almost Biblical form.

'There have been many times in my life where I have been in a state of need. It could be money, emotional rescue, worrying about an outcome of a particular situation.

'From where these Angels came that helped me I can't really say. Had I ever met these people prior to a particular incident? No. Did I ever see or meet these people after my situation had been resolved? No.

'Here's the most memorable one. Not long after 9/11, after having worked on the site at Ground Zero for three and a half weeks, I was extremely exhausted and an emotional wreck. I had lost a fair amount of capital that I had previously invested in the stock market. All music tours were cancelled. Some real estate dealings which had previously brought in a considerable amount of income had all completely ceased producing. The long and short of it was that I was running out of cash at an alarming rate. My rent at the time was $3200 per month. My expenditures and basic life overhead, including the rent, ran to about $8000 per month.

'Let's just say that living in NYC post 9/11 with zero cash coming in and no prospects of any sort of employment was starting to freak me out.

'I didn't know what to do. I could usually hustle money anywhere, doing anything. The whole city was also in a panic which didn't make the whole thing any easier.

'Here's where it gets interesting. A girlfriend of mine calls me up and asks me to help out a woman friend of hers. She asked me if I was still practicing Taoist sexual techniques. I told

Socrates • Mary Magdalen • Blessed Virgin Mary • Brunel

her I had never stopped. She recalled that I had help a sexually shutdown young lady achieve orgasm through Taoist practices.

'I know this sounds a little "out" right now. Trust me on this.

'My friend asked if I could do the same for another friend of hers. I agreed. It would be a good distraction for me. I'm about to lose everything so, fuck it! Why not. There's nothing else happening.

'Just to sum this up a bit for you. In the Taoist sexual technique, there is no physical contact of any sort. The practice involves teaching a person specific breathing and muscle controlling exercises in order to achieve full body orgasms — not just clitoral ones. Most people don't have any idea what they are missing till they get into this. It's the same as Tantric, but I like the Chinese names and descriptions much better.

'Now, my friend sets up a meet with this woman for me at a French bistro in the Village. I set out to go and meet this woman. Let's call her Mary.

'Mary and I meet. She is somewhat nervous and so I joke with her a bit in order to make her feel relaxed. We become very comfortable in each other's company and are now having a really nice time, sipping cafe au lait and enjoying some splendid French cuisine.

'After 20 minutes with her I come right out and tell her that she doesn't have ANY problems having an orgasm so let's cut the crap here. I said to her that she has a great sense of humour and is very sensual and vivacious, so I asked her, "What's this really about?"

'She said she was lonely and wanted to meet some men. We laughed and joked some more. Then we have a more honest conversation, about all sorts of stuff. We exchange cell numbers; we split up and go our separate ways.

'Two days later I get a message from Mary that she needs to

Marie Curie • *Louis Pasteur* • *Hypatia* • *Oracle of Delphi* 'gift' a certain amount of money each year and believes I could use it. I thought this strange and she assured me there were no strings attached. I questioned this whole thing thoroughly yet she assured me that it was all totally legitimate. She told me that she thought I was a very special person and that I had helped her tremendously...which is always a nice thing to hear, whatever the circumstances. Okay, I thought to myself. That was nice of her to say. At this point I was thinking she was going to send a couple of hundred or something like that.

'I gave her my address and pertinent info. A week later I wound up with $400K. Yes, you're reading correctly. $400,000.

'I tried contacting her immediately. The cell she had given me was disconnected. I never saw her again. I don't know who she was. I inquired as to how my friend knew her and she said Mary had called her and said she got her number through a mutual friend, but didn't say who this friend was. My friend called all of her friends she could think of and no one had ever heard of this Mary.

'This amount was very close to everything I had lost from my investments.

'There you have it. These type of encounters are the sort I have with what I believe to be angels. These things happen throughout my life and they are *always* very significant, if not timely. Right to the second!'

The last story in this section comes from another lady with a pseudonym, and as you read this story it'll become apparent why she has chosen to conceal her identity.

Jemima's Story

Jemima is an elegant, leggy, coltish woman in her mid-40s; a

Sir Christopher Wren • *Laurence Olivier* • *Bronwyn Bunt* • *Dante*

younger version perhaps of Joanna Lumley, with an infectious giggle and a conspiratorial, flirty air. She has a similar clipped counties accent and got in touch with me through quite a circuitous route. Her job? Some would call her a high-class hooker, but Jemima sees it a very different way.

'I was fortunate enough, whilst a naive, virginal 19 year old, to have my first sexual experiences with a beautiful Asian man who was quite a bit older than me; he was easily old enough to be my father but incredibly charismatic, if not exactly handsome in the conventional sense. It was at least a year after our first meeting before we had full penetrative sex. Prior to that, and subsequent to it, I was trained by him in some rare practices which can have the effect of giving one or both participants a transportive experience, some would say out-of-body, but for me it's as though the body, the spirit and the entire universe come together in an expansion of the senses which has no comparison to anything else. I have never in my life taken drugs or dabbled in any kind of occult practices, because I know that I have at my disposal the power, via the divine power of sexual energy, to contact angelic beings and take someone to somewhere that they are unlikely to reach any other way.

'Would I call myself a prostitute? Yes, but I think we have to look at the term with honour and with some awe. I am not a simple call-girl pulling tricks. I think of myself as a sort of sexual gatekeeper, a priestess schooled in mysteries.

I asked about the men that were her 'customers'.

'They find me via each other generally. I have relatively few clients at any one time, although the work I do is energising and invigorating and beautiful. If someone isn't in the right frame of mind for the journey I can take them on, I refuse, as diplomatically and as tactfully as possible. What I can do is not for everyone.

Lynne Lauren • *Chrissie G* • *Adam Fuest* • *Jack White*

'The angelic experiences came naturally to me, and were totally unexpected. I don't tell people exactly what to expect since it doesn't work like that. What I do, really, is akin to healing; I can shift and move the energies of the person to align with the energies of the universe that we are all a part of; if you like, I can act as a sort of tuning fork.

'The energies that I see as being the angelic energies that you're researching can take different forms for different people, but the archetypal angel, all light and wings and awesomeness, figures strongly. Sometimes when I am alone I see angels circling overhead, almost as if they are waiting to come and join in the party.

'I take what I do very, very seriously indeed. I am not able to tell people what I do; my circle of true friends and trusted people is very small. I have been referred to as a priestess. The money that I am paid is a form of energy; my talents might be given by divine forces, but my time is my own; really, the only thing that any of us ever owns. It is the time that my clients pay for and yes, before you ask, my time is expensive. Very, very expensive.

'I wish that everyone had the opportunity to experience the true nature of what sexual union is, and how much it can enhance our experience of life, and our ability to see the universe as it truly is. I know that most people go through their entire lives, having lovers, husbands, wives, children, whatever, and have no idea of what is possible, and relatively easily available to all of us.

'I see that as a great shame'.

Mind blowing stories, all of these. Again, a reminder that we can't afford to leave any possibility untried in accessing those angelic energies.

Lisa Johnson • *Sarah Gregory* • *Einstein* • *Tania Ahsan*

15

Drug Angels

Angels and Drug Culture

In the same way that that altered states of mind due to medical conditions might help us to contact the generally unseen world, deliberately-induced chemical states can also do the same thing. It's not unlikely to suppose that, in seeking out angels, you might decide to try some psychotropic substances, and whilst I'm not advocating the use of drugs either for general use or for particular means, it seems to be important to get an idea of other people's experiences, if only to give us a deeper understanding of the many different ways and means there are of making contact with the angelic realms. We can't afford to dismiss anything, since there is a very long and intriguing history of using various kinds of drugs to contact the supernatural realms.

Naturally-occurring psychedelics were traditionally the preserve of the shaman, the elders of the tribe who were initiated into the practice of ingesting certain substances in order to speak with the gods and carry their messages back to mankind. One of the most powerful of these substances is ayahuasca.

Mark Townsend · Florence Nightingale · Roald Dahl · Ernst Haas

It seems to be a bit of a buzz drug at the moment, but what exactly *is* ayahuasca? Generally prepared only by experienced shaman, it's actually a concoction of a few different ingredients which are all boiled up together. Possibly the best-known ingredient is a vine called *Banisteriopsis Caapi* (also known as yage or Caapi) which is found in Peru, Ecuador, Colombia and Western Brazil. The vine is mixed with other plants, too, which combine to make a heady brew rich in the powerful hallucinogen DMT. The other plants in question that go to make this intoxicating blend include Reed Canary Grass (*Phalaris Arundinacea*) which grows in damp areas such as banks of lakes and streams, Syrian Rue (*Peganum Harmala*) and also a mimosa species called *Jurema Preta*, as well as one of the passionflower family.

The actual strength or efficacy of the mixture is determined by the quality of the plants, the ingredients in the mixture, and above all the experience of the person 'cooking' it. It's also worth noting that some of the plants other than the banisteriopsis used in making the mixture are rich in anti-depressants known as M.A.O. inhibitors.

Although it's likely that ayahuasca has been used by indigenous shamen for hundreds, if not thousands, of years, its usage has spread throughout South America, becoming popular amongst Westerners only relatively recently. All sorts of claims are made for it; those going through the ritual have described clairvoyance, healing powers, connection with the Universe – and profoundly-affecting visions of Angels.

Here's a first-hand account from someone who has experienced the effects of ayahuasca. P is a singer with a well-known contemporary band; he's asked me not to use his real name.

'In 2007 I went with a girlfriend on one of those ayahuasca tourist things that are getting popular. It's not the way I'd have wanted to

Ansel Adams • *Simone Johnson* • *Alan Card* • *Mike H* • *Judika Illes*

be introduced to this substance, to be honest, but I was keen to do it in its country of origin, so to speak. So there we are in Peru.

'The ritual itself is interesting. You've got to go on a sort of detox diet beforehand, probably to prime your mind as well as your body for the rites. I don't eat meat or much dairy anyway, which is definitely a bonus, since it makes the detoxing experience easier.

'Anyway, we're out in the middle of the jungle with the shaman and we drink an oily black liquid. We're warned that we might get the heaves - that's part of the detox process going on. This wasn't so bad for me but the girl I was with was seriously ill. But then she was a die-hard McDonald's girl!

'The first thing that I started to enjoy (after the vomiting) and to really take notice of was the music. The shaman and his crew were singing some kinds of songs; every note seemed to be slowed-down, surreal, and sort of bell-like in its clarity. It was really beautiful...The notes corresponded to colours, too, and everything opened up into a sort of internal/external rainbow that I became a part of. I seemed to be somehow expanding outside of my little self and becoming a part of everything; I felt a deep, deep sense of both peace and excitement at the same time. Just telling you about all this triggers the memory of those feelings which I hope will never go away.

'Then I started to feel as though I was floating, or flying. This was the most amazing, beautiful experience. Although I felt as though I was on my own, I was also related to everyone else on the trip, then everyone else in the country, and then every soul in the entire universe seemed to be joined up like tiny points of light. I don't know if I'm conveying this feeling very well, but I felt as though I was an aeroplane that had come to land perfectly on the runway; everything lined up effortlessly and I knew who I was without my ego being involved – does that make sense?

All the contributors to this book • *James Lebon* • *Joni Mitchell*

'Then, the best thing and the thing that has stayed with me, is that in my floaty journey I came into what can only be described as a huge crowd of angels, of whom I was included. I was a part of the intense brightness and I've known since then that angels actually do exist; it's an unshakeable knowledge rather than just a feeling, but I'm aware that it might sound daffy to anyone that hasn't had the same experience; it's as though I'd lived in some kind of cave until that point.

'At one part of the journey I was aware of the shaman. He had become a being of intense brightness, with huge wings like a bird, another angel-form almost too bright to look at. He was tiny but huge, too, as big as the planet and as small as a mouse; I went back and read descriptions of angels to see what tallied up with my experience and this hugeness/tininess, i.e. "the normal rules do not apply" thing seems to be a part of the general description.

'I guess ayahuasca showed me the universe as it really is, and that I experienced things in a way that wouldn't work in the everyday lives that we have to live in. But I know one thing for sure; I know that angels are real and that they're all over the place'.

Possibly the best-known hallucinogenic drug in the UK and other parts of Europe, which is relatively freely-available and which occurs naturally, are 'magic mushrooms'. There are other types of fungi that produce psychotropic effects, such as the amanita mascara or fly agaric, but the small psilocybin mushrooms, also known as 'liberty caps', are the ones that are generally termed 'magic'. Here's an account which has some similarities to the ayahuasca story but without the same elaborate rituals. Cathy is a painter and illustrator who has worked on several books. The following incident took place some ten years ago, when she was still a student.

Rhona Heath · *Bobby Osborne* · *The Penponties* · *Lewis Carroll*

Cathy Takes a Trip with the Angels

'I had a boyfriend back at that time who was a bit older and more experienced in many aspects of life than I, and I was very much in love with him, and he with me. At this time, I have to tell you I was very innocent of anything to do with drugs. I'd never actually taken anything at all apart from the odd aspirin! I'd never smoked dope, never wanted to snort or inject or do anything to alter the state of my mind; weird maybe for an art student, but that's the way I was. Possibly a bit over-cautious!

'Anyway, one time we went camping in Sussex. It was late September, and my boyfriend told me that it was a great time for magic mushrooms. I decided to stop being such a prude and give it a go; I trusted him implicitly and I knew he'd never advocate anything that would harm me in any way.

'So he showed me which mushrooms we were meant to look for; they're tiny with little pointy tops like pixie hats. They were growing in a field with quite a lot of long grass, but once you knew what you were looking for they were very easy to find, and there were lots of them.

'Steve made them into a tea, and we drank half each. I lay with my feet in the tent and my upper torso out of it, wrapped in a blanket, and waited for something to happen.

'At first it seemed as though nothing at all was happening, and then I realised that my perspective was gradually starting to shift, like looking at something through old glass; colours were sharpening, sounds were slowing down and becoming more exaggerated. As an artist, it proved to be a pretty useful experience and I suddenly felt that I knew some of the influence of all those great '60s and '70s album sleeves!

'Everything seemed to be pulsating, as though everything was joined and a part of everything else. I was a part of this

Zoroaster • *John Dee* • *Nancy Palmer-Jones* • *Adam Fuest*

much, much bigger picture; the rhythm of 'me', the Cathy part of me, was at one with the universe and shared its rhythm.

'I was staring at the blades of grass outside the tent. My face was close to the grass, something I hadn't done since I was a kid, when I used to squint at the blades through strong sunlight, make them change shape, go fuzzy and alter the colours.

'One blade of grass in particular was super real. There was a drop of water on the side of it and as I looked into this tiny drop, into its rainbows, I saw that it encompassed an angel, the most beautiful thing you've ever seen; a classical angel, archetypal, but tiny, suspended in this dewdrop.

'I felt overwhelmed, and I suddenly understood everything. This experience was effectively small, and easy to dismiss as the product of having taken the mushrooms, but it was also very huge and very important, and the essence of that complete understanding has stayed with me – I know it's there, but it's not always appropriate in our everyday lives to have that kind of intensity.

'My boyfriend didn't experience anything quite so deep; he had taken mushrooms, and other drugs, many times before. I do wonder if my experience was more profound because I hadn't ever taken any drugs before. And weirdly enough, I guess, I've never done it again. The experience was so exquisite that I've never felt the need to repeat it.

'An angel, suspended in a dewdrop, on a blade of grass in a field in Sussex. Beautiful. And totally real'.

While not advocating the use of drugs, it is very interesting to compare the different encounters that these people have had with angels whilst under the influence of certain substances. This last story is from Mark, (not his real name) a guitarist with a band that were popular in the 1990s.

Jeanne McKenzie • *Robert Atherton* • *Doreen Virtue* • *Jacqui Newcombe*

'I think I was pretty innocent as far as drugs went. In fact I know I was, compared to some of the people around me. I just wasn't really interested and for that I count myself lucky when I see what's happened to a lot of the people that were around back then, and what they've become for lack of discipline and total indulgence in some really nasty stuff. But I did have a really amazing, beautiful experience the first time I ever took any drugs at all. It's almost shameful to tell you this was in Amsterdam, but hey-ho, there you go.

'We were there to do a couple of gigs, and a bit of promo, TV and radio, that sort of stuff. There was a lot of pressure on me because everyone was into the cafes and the idea of doing any kind of drugs just really wasn't me. I resisted till the day before the end of the whole tour, when we had some time off.

'I'd met this really lovely German girl. It wasn't a boyfriend/girlfriend thing, just a mates thing, although we got a lot of teasing; it really wasn't like that, it was more of a brother/sister vibe. I'll call her Susanna. Susanna knew I wasn't into the drugs thing but I did want to try something – seemed rude not to and we were certainly in the place for it. We were sitting by a quiet stretch of canal when she handed me a piece of cake. She broke it and we ate half each like; I felt like a character in *Alice in Wonderland*.

'The whole thing was lovely and mellow and not at all frightening. Susanna sort of talked to me, talked me through what was happening, and because of what she told me I started to see angels drifting over the water of the canal, not conventional angels like you'd expect to see, but rainbow forms with human faces and drifty wings that flowed behind them. It felt as though they were something to do with the spirit of the water. And there was music that came with them – mixed up with all the other sounds that were going on but like an ethereal

Diana Cooper · *The Prophet* · *Roald Dahl* · *Paulo Coelho*

string section right out there in the distance, with instruments that sounded familiar but which I couldn't quite put a finger on. That music never left me – I tried to score it and got somewhere close, but it was not quite the same. The whole thing was beautiful, but I didn't want to try to repeat it. It was a once-in-a-lifetime thing. I never told any of the guys in the band because I knew that their experiences were totally different, probably much more "earthy" and indulgent, and I didn't want to spoil what had happened by trying to explain'.

Jesus Christ • *Jeremy Clarkson* • *Patti Smith* • *Tim Smit*

16

Rock and Roll Angels

Angelic energies and creative energies are closely linked, and I believe it's extremely likely that they're exactly the same thing. It stands to reason, then, that people involved in the creative arts will have had direct experience of being inspired by sources that seem, at the same time, to be outside themselves and yet a part of themselves. In the same way that the healer allows angelic energies to flow through his or her body, allowing him or herself to be used as a vessel for these supernatural energies, so it is that some artists and musicians, particularly when liberated from the moment by technical expertise that has become second nature, can access powers and energies that are 'other' and which stand outside the conventional boundaries of time.

One of the most famous contemporary relationships between a musician and an angel is that between Carlos Santana and the Angel that inspires his work, Metatron. We'll take a look at this cosmic relationship in a moment, but the fact that Santana is ready to speak so openly about this cosmic collaboration is even more remarkable in view of some things that should be pointed out.

Anita Roddick • *Alexandra David-Neal* • *Dalai Lama*

Why is it that, in this country, we are so often afraid to be honest about certain aspects of our spirituality? Why are we so keen to categorise, to keep one of the most important facets of our lives under wraps, in its 'proper' place, not a part of everyday life?

Travel to any of the Eastern countries and you'll see that spirituality is an open part of life. For example, in Bali and other parts of Indonesia you'll see beautiful offerings of flowers, fruit and the wafting smoke of scented incense carefully arranged on leaves or small dishes, places at corners and intersections as an acknowledgment to the spirits of the place.

Hindu temples in India are exuberant, noisy places where ritual worship and everyday life interact, each an essential part of the other. The spontaneous music, children running around, people draping the colourful flower *malas* over statues and effigies and the odd chicken or dog wandering about does not in the least detract from the inherent respect accorded to a sacred space. Put in context, you can understand why there was such a burgeoning interest in Eastern philosophies, most famously demonstrated by the Beatles, during the generational shift in spiritual awareness which took place in the Flower Power era of the 1960s.

Then there's a Buddhist sanctuary in Kathmandu, Swayam-bunath, which is full of monkeys running around all over the place, since the animal, like all other animals, is considered to be sacred here. Compare this to the UK, where even a dog on a leash inside most churches would be looked at askance for most of the year.

What's wrong with us? What are we afraid of?

In the same way, we tend to treat those public figures who dare to talk about spirituality – outside of the designated Sunday morning and evening slots of radio and television – as slightly ditsy. Unless, of course, there's a personal tragedy involved, in

Barack Obama • *Jules Verne* • *Frances Drake* • *Dylan Thomas*

which case we are quick to 'ooh' and 'aah' over any titillating revelations in the glossy pages of the celebrity magazines on the shelves of our newsagents and supermarkets.

If the important public figures in our lives declare themselves religiously or spiritually affiliated, there's a tendency to think that they're a bit 'touched'. One, for having the belief in the first place. And two, for committing the unpardonable sin of actually *talking* about it!

Forever after, these people are tainted with a reputation for being a bit 'odd'. And yet we are fascinated by them and their stories; we allow them to carry into the open that part of ourselves that many of us prefer to remain secret.

'*...I'd rather live with my craziness than your sane realities!*'
—CARLOS SANTANA

It's always refreshing when figures in the public eye talk freely about spiritual matters. Maybe it's no accident that the people that *can* get away with declaring their beliefs and allegiances, however, are those involved in the arts in some way, the people that we call 'creatives'. We almost expect these people to be 'different'. But why? And this raises the question; are angels more likely to be attracted to creative energies, or are those with creative energies more liable to be consciously attracted to angels and angelic energies?

A good example of this is Carlos Santana, the Mexican megastar, a virtuoso guitarist who has sold millions of albums during his long and successful career. Santana not only freely acknowledges the presence of angels, but communicates with one of the most powerful of all; Metatron, who is also known as the Angel of the Face since this particular Angel is said to be the only one that can actually look upon the face of God.

Robbie Burns • *T.S. Eliot* • *Jeremy Sandford* • *Bruce Chatwin*

Santana is an intriguing character. Born into impoverished circumstances in Autlan ne Navarro in 1947, by the time he was 12 and the family had relocated to Tijuana, he was already playing in the local nightclubs after he swapped his violin for a guitar. He was interested in the soulful expressions of musicians such as John Coltrane and Ray Charles. However, when the family moved once more, to San Francisco, the musical world opened up, figuratively speaking, with a clash of cymbals and a huge drum roll, and he encountered a range of different styles. It was whilst he was working as a dishwasher that he was fortunate enough to be mentored by The Grateful Dead's Jerry Garcia, who encouraged him to form his own group; Santana.

It's apparent how vastly the music business has changed when you consider that when Santana played to a half a million people at the Woodstock festival in 1969, there was no sign of a recording contract and he wasn't supported by any record labels. This came after a television appearance on the Ed Sullivan show.

These were heady times, dangerous for some. Santana enjoyed all the delights that the prevailing breeze of the hedonistic '60s and early '70s could bring; his eponymous debut album sold four million copies and appeared in the Billboard charts for two years, and all Santana's albums continue to sell today. However, the drug-related deaths of Janis Joplin, Jim Morrison and Jimi Hendrix caused the young Carlos to become more circumspect and he turned away from substances and towards spirituality as a means of coping with his high-pressure life. He embraced the teachings of a guru, Sri Chinmoy, and renamed himself Devadip, meaning 'light of the lamp of the Supreme'.

So, in Carlos Santana we have someone who is creative; who is manifesting that creativity in music; and who is open to spiritual beliefs and ideals.

Beryl Nozedar • *Trevor Nozedar* • *Andrew Catlin* • *Edith Piaf*

He speaks extensively about his experience with angels – and in particular, of Metatron, in Rolling Stone magazine. This is a good example of how we might sometimes seem to get a 'calling', and it's up to us – and depending on our state of attunement at the time – whether we follow that calling or not.

Here's what happened in Santana's case.

In 1988, in Milwaukee airport, he was drawn to buy a paperback about angels, probably in much the same way that you decided to buy the book that you are now reading. This small action was the beginning of an increasing fascination and culminates in actual contact with Metatron, of whom Santana says:

'Metatron is the architect of all physical life. Because of him, we can French kiss, we can hug, we can get a hot dog, we can wiggle a toe'.

The first time that Metatron communicated directly with Santana was at a meditation group in Santa Cruz, California. He was told: 'You will be inside the radio frequency for the purpose of connecting the molecules with the light'.

For Santana, this meant that his music would be heard on the radio, and sure enough, the molecules *did* connect with the light. Santana is keen to talk about such matters and uses his fame to spread his message and to talk about the things that he believes are important: 'I don't care, man, what anybody thinks about my reality. My reality is that God speaks to you every day. There's an inner voice, and when you hear it, you get a little tingle in the medulla oblongata at the back of your neck, a little shiver, and at two o' clock in the morning, when everything's really quiet and you got the candles, you got the incense and you've been chanting, and all of a sudden you hear this voice; WRITE THIS DOWN. It's just an inner voice, and you trust it. That voice will never take you to the desert'.

The other advice that Metatron imparted to Santana was this:

Billie Holiday • *James Watt* • *Louis Armstrong* • *The Searys*

'Be patient, be gracious, be grateful'. This is good advice, and we'll look in more depth at the Gratitude Attitude in Part 2 of this book.

Santana meets his angelic presence half way, too. Where he lives in San Rafael, California, he has two properties. One property is the family home where he lives with his wife and three children. The other property is what Santana names his Church. Here, at his meditation spot facing the fireplace, Santana burns that incense and enjoys the flickering of candles, and transcribes the messages that are sent to him by his angelic friend. (Again, we'll look at making a space for angels in the second part of this book).

It's not only Carlos Santana that recognises the help that comes from the angelic realms. Here's a short anecdote from Bobby Harlow, lead singer with Detroit's The Go.

Bobby's Story

'I was driving down the expressway in a full size Dodge van. I must have been travelling at a speed of around 70mph, and it was rush hour, so I was surrounded by automobiles (at top speed).

'It was winter, and freezing out, but the roads seemed clear. The van hit a large patch of ice and began to slide. Everything went slow-mo and the entire van slid 90 degrees, so I was facing the driver's side door of the car in the lane next to me. I actually thought, "When the ice ends, and the van hits dry pavement, I'm going to flip and die."

'In an instant, my mind visualized the conclusion and it was grim. Suddenly, it felt as though somebody reached out of the sky and grabbed hold of the top of the van. The entire vehicle was turned straight around and placed back on track.

'I just sat behind the wheel, navigating on auto-pilot. Both

Theo   Chalmers   •   Janet   Gleghorn   •   Edmund   Hilary

the passenger and I were stunned, speechless, and bewildered. It just didn't make sense. How did this happen?!

'Well, I'm still convinced: Somebody reached out of the sky and set me back on course. This happens to me all of the time…not quite as dramatically, thankfully'.

Douglas Bader • Elvis • Grace Darling • Rosa Parks

17

Angels of the iPod?

'This might sound crazy, but I think I get angelic messages from my iPod when I put it on shuffle tracks. I've been going through some 'interesting times' lately and the lyrics that pop up seem to have an extraordinary relevance to my situation. Is that possible?'

—JOE, 27

I don't see why not. I think this makes a lot of sense! Mark Townsend, whose story appears earlier, has a good argument for 'signs' appearing on the sides of lorries and other vehicles. We'll look at the mysteries of angelic energies and synchronicity in a little while.

Music of the Spheres?

Pythagoras posited a theory that every planet in our solar system resonated to a certain frequency; further, that there was not only the music made by instruments, but also tones for the human body and soul. All these frequencies, he said, resonated with one another in mathematical harmony to make the Music of the Spheres, or *Musica Universalis*. Some people believe that it

Christian Barnard • Simon Clayton • Esti Clayton • Linda and Dominic

is actually possible, sometimes, to detect this music. Karen Frandsen may well be one of these people.

Karen's Story

As well as being a fine artist, Karen Frandsen and her partner Ian run a documentary film production team called "Eerie Investigations", which, as the name suggests, documents all matters esoteric, supernatural and paranormal. Their shows are aired five days a week on one of the satellite channels.

Karen had a fortunate upbringing in that the child's natural affinity with the unseen world, so often discouraged after the age of seven or so, was never drummed out of her; her mother was psychic, and so when the same gifts started to reveal themselves in the young Karen they were actively encouraged. In fact, the realm of interesting and extraordinary experiences that Karen has had would probably fill a book all on their own. Here's her story.

'About 12 years ago, I don't know if you remember, it seemed a time when everything started to speed up, one of those generational periods of enlightenment that sweeps many people up, advances their spiritual development.

'One evening I was just going to bed. It was about twenty minutes past eleven, and Ian was cleaning his teeth in the bathroom next door. It was a warm summer solstice evening and as I lay down on the pillow, I suddenly heard some really beautiful choral music.

'I said to Ian, "Where's that music coming from, can you hear that?" He said that he couldn't. I thought it was a bit odd that he couldn't hear something that was so clear, but didn't think too much of it at the time. I opened the window and looked out; I couldn't see anything that would tell me where the music was

Marco Polo • *Alex Maiolo* • *Stanley Meyer* • *Nikola Tesla*

coming from. So I went downstairs and opened the back door to see if it was coming from the other side of the house.

'As I looked out of the back door, it dawned on me that the music wasn't actually coming from any specific direction; it was just sort of hanging in the air. It's at that point that I thought, "Aha...this isn't ordinary music!"

'I then rang a couple of friends who are also psychic, to see if maybe they were hearing it too, or whether they might have an explanation to offer. I also phoned my sister. She said, "It sounds as though 'something' is going to happen, and music is heralding this 'something'".

'So, I went to sleep with this fabulous music going on. I noted that it wasn't in my head, but definitely from an external source.

'The next morning, the music was gone. But as I was pegging the washing out at around 9.30, it started again. Very excited, I called Ian at work to tell him; he took it in his stride, since he's used to odd things happening around me from time to time. It stopped again an hour later, at about 10.30. Then it started again just after lunch, at about 2.30. And ever since then it's been with me all the time.

'It doesn't bother me at all; it's very beautiful. But the really interesting thing is that whenever anything "big" is going to happen, it changes tempo and increases in volume. One good example is when Diana, Princess of Wales, died. It started increasing in volume from about a week beforehand, and of course her death rocked the world. After she died, the level of the music dropped down to normal again.

'The tsunami of late 2004 was another big incident that was heralded in the same way, by the increase in volume and tempo of the music. I'm warned about plane crashes, earthquakes, things like that. I can't actually discern what exactly is going to happen from the music alone, though.

Lynne Lauren • *Tylluan Penry* • *Bill Gates* • *Warren Buffett*

'I did ask once "why me?" and received an answer back; "Because you're listening!"

'If you want to get an idea of what this music sounds like, it's sort of a cross between "Agnus Dei" by Barber, and Enya's musical piece called "Eclipse" very dreamy and choral.

'I believe that what I am hearing is the phenomenon that Pythagoras called the "Music of the Spheres". Maybe I am tuning into the song of the universe.

'One evening, some months after it had started, myself, my husband Ian, my cousin, my sister and a friend were sitting relaxing at home with some background music playing on the stereo. All of us, with the exception of my sister, had recently received Reiki 1 and 2 attunements. We were busy talking and didn't immediately notice that the CD on the stereo had finished.

'I suddenly became very aware – because of the looks on their faces, they were all in a strange kind of shock – that Ian, my cousin, and my friend were still hearing music, the same music that I was hearing! I said to them, "You can hear the music, can't you?" They all nodded, realising at the same time that the stereo was not playing and that the music they could hear was "mine" Each of them said that they heard it for a couple of minutes before it faded, the exception being my sister who didn't hear anything.

'What is even stranger is that my friend later read her horoscope for that weekend and it said "This weekend you will share in someone's cosmic gift".'

Interestingly, Karen mentioned that she had just started her Reiki training when the music started. Of all the healing practices, it has been reiki practitioners who made the most numerous responses to my appeal for stories for this book.

Prof Alan Jones • *Phillip Carr-Gomm* • *Stephanie Carr-Gomm*

18
Angels in a Real Emergency
The terrorist attack of 7/7

We've talked about how angels appear at times of extreme stress. Here, angels appear during a time of extreme danger, too.

The following is an extraordinary account of the tube bombings in London on July 7, 2007.

Beverli's Story

'When you come face to face with the greatness of the angels, and the power and energy that they have, it seems to automatically create tears'

Beverli Rhodes is one of the survivors of the 7/7 terrorist attacks, when bombs were set off on the London Underground. The majority of us have fortunately never experienced such a colossal trauma so it's hard to comprehend exactly what an effect such an event could have on one's life. Everything turned upside down for Beverli, and she was affected physically,

Yuri Gagarin • Buddy Holly • Ennio Morricone

emotionally, financially; she has spent months in and out of hospitals as far away as Thailand, was made redundant from her work, and yet her attitude is utterly inspirational. When she talks you get a sense that this is one woman who truly can be described as 'indomitable.' She was told that she would never ride again and defied both the opinion of the doctors and all logical thought and is now on horseback most days. She is funny, courageous, and determined, and has turned her life around after the devastation rent by the attack. Her spiritual journey, too, has been profound and extraordinary. Beverli's story has lessons for us all. Here it is.

'I know that, because of the blast, my memories of the actual event tend to be a bit scattered, but there are certain aspects which have intense clarity.

'Ironically, when the blast happened I was on my way to the Olympic offices. London had been confirmed as host city for the 2012 Olympics just the day before, and I was on my way to consultancy offices to a meeting regarding the Olympics with Olympic Delivery Authorities – and guess what, we were due to begin discussions about the security logistics!

'I was knocked unconscious by the blast; apparently I was out for a good ten minutes. When I came to I was aware not only of the people around me but of the circumstances. It was obvious what must have happened. In a situation like the one I was in, it's amazing how quickly and how effectively your survival mechanisms kick in. For example, the air was thick with acrid smoke and it was second nature to get down close to the floor of the carriage where the air was cleaner. A part of your brain is calm and clear, telling you what to do. It was also instinctive to start praying, and I found myself in amongst a group, all women, who prayed together in whatever way was the most

David Lynch • Amy Johnson • Donald Campbell • Amelia Earhart

natural to us; all different languages, all different beliefs, all with the same reaction to appeal to some sort of a higher source. Don't they say that the most extreme atheist becomes a believer at the death bed?

'It's funny that it was the women praying whilst the men were trying to find a way out of the situation. It was a mixture of practical and spiritual skills that seemed equally necessary. But we thought we were going to die, we really did; and that's when the angels appeared.

'They were huge, very, very big, wraith-like and dreamy, beings of light, sexless, with long fingers. I assumed it was the angels that were coming to take us away, that we were dying. There was a real human angel too – a big burly bloke who looked like a Hells Angel type, quite scary; he broke all the joints in his fingers trying to pry open one of the doors, but since they had all gone into 'lock' mode when the bomb went off, his efforts were in vain.

'The process of praying to these visible angels was, for me, incredibly liberating. I have been a Buddhist for 20 years, and I prayed for light, assistance, compassion. I went over my life and did meditations of release, saying thanks for the opportunity to be on this planet, for the lessons that I had learned, and being a part of lessons that others had learned from. I thought about all my relatives, friends, husband and children, and released them. I knew that they would be upset by my death, but I also knew that they were strong enough to cope. This experience, the feeling of detachment, and the realisation that I was going freely and unencumbered to what I thought would be my death, I feel now was a great privilege. This experience is not available to everyone and I do feel very fortunate to know what it feels like, and to know for sure that there's nothing to be afraid of. The more we prayed the more noticeable and defined the angelic beings became.

John Morris • Ron Edwards • David Lynch • Henry Miller

'Why did we expect to die? Well, there was live electricity on the tracks. The smoke was choking and acrid. People were already bleeding to death. And with this heightened awareness I could see that people's souls were leaving their bodies as balls of light; some of them were met by similar balls of light, and the two balls merged and floated off together. Other souls left alone, and my perception of this was that these souls needed to go into some kind of a holding pattern for some reason.

'For me, I felt intense peace. I did a mental shopping list of all the things in my life that were left undone, and then I let them go, with thanks. In my mind, I told everyone that I loved them, and apologised for the few things which might have been left unsaid. I made peace with all the things that were wrong. I wasn't afraid to die.

'The striking thing that I remember was the familiar feeling about the angels; it was like meeting old friends that you haven't seen for ages and have almost forgotten about. The situation changed gradually, and I suddenly realised that I was actually alive, and that I was going to live. It might sound crazy, but this information was given to me by the angels. I found that I could communicate with them; it was as though I had thoughts and questions in my mind that didn't come out of my mouth, and which didn't need to be said out loud.

'Yes, I have changed since this experience. In fact, everything changed, some things more gradually than others. I had changed, too. I had had experiences and seen things which I needed to integrate, to 'normalise' my life somehow after everything had been turned upside down. Exactly a month after the blast, I was made redundant from work. I can understand why they had to make this decision and I have no problems with it. The first thing that I had to consider was my own physical recovery. Many of the procedures that I needed to have to fix my

Doug and Joy • *Ellen Macarthur* • *Jont* • *Oppenheimer*

body were not available in the UK, and I had to sell things to be able to afford the medical treatments that I needed in Thailand. I sold my car, the jewellery that my husband and children had given me. I considered that I was lucky to have these things to sell, and any thoughts of sentimental value went straight out of the window'.

I asked Beverli whether she had had any further experiences of angels since her experience on 7/7.

'Yes – I have. I became aware that I had a feeling of something angelic that was around me, so one day I decided to see if I could again communicate with it, as I had during that day on the Underground. This presence definitely felt like a he and he told me his name; Uriel. I had never heard this name before but when I looked it up I found that Uriel is the angel that rules over people that are born on a Wednesday. Uriel is also the bringer of divine justice. I know that this being has been with me since day one, and funnily enough a few months ago I had a short contract to do a piece of integrative work as one company was taking over another.

'The staff were all very angry, and I quickly realised that this was because they were being treated like pieces of equipment or machinery, not like human beings, during the course of the take-over. My role was to be able to audit the situation as dispassionately as possible, to see both sides of the situation and bring about a resolution.

'Since I knew that I had Uriel's powers as bringer of divine justice on my side, I approached the problem with this energy in my mind. There was a queue at my door at all times during this job, from both sides of the problem, and I decided to ask the staff members not to be angry, but to see their situation as a

Freud • Jung • You • Picasso • Lyn and Margaret Regan

chance to evolve, to see the bigger picture and the context in which these changes were happening. After all, what's the worst thing that could happen? It had already happened to me, so I could speak from a position of authority! Even after the contract was over, I am still in touch with over half the people that I dealt with. I am glad that I enabled change in their lives. Being able to help people find their own path and reconnect them with their self-worth is a fantastic privilege.

'I had another very profound experience. I was having tests at a hospital in Bangkok, and had a couple of hours to kill whilst I waited for the results. There was a temple just down the road, and so I decided to go there to pass the time.

'It's funny how things can happen, seemingly in a random manner. At the temple, there was a specific sort of ritual going on, something like soul retrieval. Because partner and I are blonde and obviously westerners, everyone was staring at us, and although we were made to feel very welcome we were definitely under close scrutiny.

'The ritual involved a blessing over a bowl of water, which then had to be taken very carefully over to the banyan tree – which is sacred in the Buddhist tradition – and poured into the ground at the base of the tree. As the water was being blessed, I was thinking of the very many people that I wanted to include in the blessing. I took the water to the tree, and as I watched, the drops changed from being mere water and transformed into glittering, tiny, celestial beings. It was so beautiful. The tears were running down my face, unbidden, unconsciously. The monk passed someone a small Buddha in a glass case to give to me; I was completely blown away. This experience was on a par with the one I had of the angels on the Underground that day.

'At the hospital, they had discovered that I had a tumour on my lung. This was as a result of breathing in the toxic fumes that were

Me • Ptolemy • JK Rowling • JRR Tolkien

given off during the blast. They were worried that the presence of the tumour would be affected by the other surgical procedures that I needed, and would make breathing difficult, but I insisted that they go ahead. The CEO of the hospital came to see me and gave me several options for the removal of the tumour, but I had a little voice inside me that simply told me to refuse any treatment for it whatsoever. I knew that this was a big test.

'During the surgery, I floated out of my body and looked back at myself. I looked dreadful; my eyes were taped over, I had Vaseline all over my face, tubes coming out of my mouth. As I looked back at myself, laughing, I became aware of different levels of angels around me, almost like a hierarchy. I knew that Uriel had brought them in to watch over me. I asked; are you going to help deal with the tumour? The reply was yes, that I didn't need to worry about it. The angels were all different colours, some golden, some silvery; they were defined by the light that they gave out. I was aware that many of them had been physicians or healers for many, many years or for many lifetimes.

'The funny bit happened after the operation. I came to, lying on the little narrow trolley in the recovery room just outside the operating theatre. Uriel was still there, and I tried to get off the trolley to follow him, and had to be put back by the nurses!

'Since then, the tumour has shrunk so much that it no longer needs to be monitored and no action needs to be taken. The last time I saw the consultant he could hardly believe his eyes; I still have all the CT slice lung plates, which effectively provide photographic evidence. Then the CEO of the hospital came to see me and chased everyone out of the room, so he could tell me a story in privacy.

'He said, in slightly broken English, "I tell you story about me. I have once seven of these tumours. I ask Lord Buddha to take away, and he takes away."'

Pablo Casals • *Jaqueline DuPrey* • *Maria Callas* • *Carl Sagan*

Today, Beverli may still have many medical problems, but the determination and fortitude with which she has turned her life around are truly remarkable. She takes her beautiful horses to events all over the UK and is a fit, healthy, beautiful and talented woman. Indeed, she has been touched by angels.

Jonathan Cainer • Dame Margot Fonteyn • Nureyev • The Heathies Ghandi

19

Guardian Angels
Angels of Tough Love?

'*Every blade of grass has over it an angel saying, "grow".*'
—THE TALMUD

'*Every raindrop that falls is accompanied by an angel, for every raindrop is a manifestation of being.*'
—THE QUR'AN

'*...My friends constantly assure me I'm going to be okay, that they're on my side and they're my allies. They tell me they are my guardian angels and they will help me through it.*'
—BRIAN WILSON, THE BEACH BOYS

And so what of the guardian angel, perhaps the most popular angelic manifestation of all?

The idea that every single one of us — every single living person on the planet — has a guardian angel to watch over us, mentor us, and guide us through both calm and stormy seas from our first breath to our last, is an appealing one to many people and, as we can see from the quotes above, transcends the barriers of race, culture and religious belief. But did you know

• Stephen Hawking • Mother Teresa • Peter Sellers

that it's not only human beings that have the privilege of help from such a friend? The original Guardian Angel of the Planet Earth was Satan, for example – hence his personification as material forces in the 15th card of the Major Arcana of the Tarot. The Earth is of course the material plane in which we live, essentially the opposite of the spirit world.

We don't need to use the term guardian angel, either, if we don't want to. To the Romans, it was called the Genius; a Shaman might call is the Spirit Helper; Arabs might call it the Genii. Poets, artists and writers often call it the Muse. It's interesting that highly-driven creative people seem to have a deeper relationship with this entity than many other people, often suffering great hardships in the name of their art. The artistic muse can be a cruel mistress.

The concept of the guardian angel isn't actually mentioned as such in the Bible, although in the gospel of Matthew, Jesus advises the disciples that every child has its angel in Heaven, which might bear some similarity to the idea. In Christian culture it first appears in the 13th century in the *Summa Theologica*, written by St Thomas Aquinas.

Elsewhere, in the Jewish Mystery Tradition of the Kabbalah, we're told that there are four ruling princes of the Guardian Angel squads, and that there are 70 angels assigned to guard all the nations of the Earth, although what happens when political boundaries are altered isn't explained. What's also not always explained is that these seven can apparently be either 'angels or demons', according to a learned text by Buber, entitled *Tales of the Hasidim Early Masters*. We can guess that these angels might have become corrupted by close contact with the material forces of the Earth – all, that is, except for Michael, one of our 'Big Three' angels, who has jurisdiction over Jerusalem and the 'chosen people'. We can see a political angle at work here, as

Tony Benn • *Joanna Lumley* • *Keir Hardie* • *T E Lawrence*

well as taking such an interpretation at a more literal level; that perhaps angels and demons have more in common than we might like to imagine.

Expanding on the idea that we each have our own guardian angel, the Talmud asserts that every Jewish person is assisted throughout his or her life by not one but 11,000 such entities.

There are countless stories of intervention by our own guardian angels; a quick flick through a book search online revealed at least 50 on the market right now. And a lot of the stories are incredibly similar, which would seem to lend credence to their veracity. I'm sure you know the sort of thing. We find the guardian angel reappearing again and again in tales of popular folklore, where they whisk people away from danger at the last second, manifesting as a physical tug from behind and saving us from being run over by trains, cars and lorries.

I think there's something more to it than this, though. Let's look at things in another way. What if the concept of the fluffy guardian angel isn't quite as its always depicted?

Remember that, with all things angelic, we always have to 'unexpect the expected'. Anthony Peake, in his book *The Daemon*, posits the idea that each of us has another 'self' that has experienced this life before, and is occasionally able to break through in order to communicate something to us, whether it is a warning, a reminder, or an idea. Peake offers the notion that the feeling of déjà vu might be a sign that the Daemon is at work. Peake's theory nods towards the much older concept of the Greek daemon which equates to the notion of our latter day guardian angel. Apuleius said that daemons inhabited the air, were transparent and therefore invisible, but that they could sometimes be heard. Like birds, the fact that the daemons inhabit the element of air implies that they can come and go between the material and spiritual realms, and again like birds,

Richard Burton • *Finlay, Janette and Tyler* • *George Harrison*

the daemon carries the same task of carrying messages to and from these two worlds. This also accords with the Sufi idea of angels.

Historically speaking, perhaps the most famous daemon of the ancient world was that belonging to the great philosopher Socrates. It seems this particular daemon was a succinct character; his sole intervention was to say a loud 'No' whenever his charge was either in danger or about to do something offensive to the gods. It's said that those of us with a particularly striking vocation or mission on this Earth are sometimes fortunate enough to have a particularly clear and focussed idea of who their daemon is, and how it looks. The great psychologist, C.G. Jung, is a good example. He had a strange dream, of an old man with the horns of a bull, flying through the sky. The old man was clutching four keys in such a way that it looked as though he was going to open a lock with one of the keys. In this way, through the mechanism of a dream, Jung's personal daemon revealed itself.

Jung's daemon even revealed his name; Philemon. He visited Jung not only in dreams, but in his waking hours too. In *Memories, Dreams, Reflections*, the memoir that was published in 1961, Jung writes:

'At times he seemed to me quite real, as if he were a living personality. I went walking up and down the garden with him, and to me he was what the Indians call a guru... Philemon brought home to me the crucial insight that there are things in the psyche which I do not produce, but which have their own life...I held conversations with him and he said things which I had not consciously thought...He said I treated thoughts as if I generate them myself but in his view thoughts were like animals in the forest, or people in a room...It was he who taught me psychic objectivity, the reality of the psyche.'

Terry Gilliam • David Lean • Michelangelo • Jim Morrison

Plotinus, too, gives a lot of advice in regard to our personal daemon. He said that if we choose to live well, then we go to a higher level, and we are accordingly given a higher-level daemon. The more consciously we aim to perfect our lives, the higher we rise with our daemons, which are both within us and outside of us. Interestingly, it seems that by listening to this inner voice we allow it, too, to develop spiritually; there's a symbiosis between the two, a partnership.

Plato, in *The Republic*, tells the story of a man called Er, who seems to have had what we'd now term a near-death experience. He brought back news not only of what happens when we die and afterwards, but from the opposite end of the spectrum; what happens before we are born. We might think that the idea that we choose everything in our lives – even our parents – before we were born – is a modern one, but this certainly isn't the case. Er learned that we choose the lives that we are about to embark on, and that we are also allotted a personal guide to help us manifest that choice. After the course of our lives has been fixed, we then pass into life on this plane and we are born. Effectively, according to Er, our daemon – or guardian angel, remember – holds a sort of map or blueprint of our lives. It's the Daemon that calls us to our true vocation and which provides the 'still small voice' inside that tells us whether we are doing right or wrong. This personal daemon is impersonal in that it does not get caught up in the emotional world of the human being, but is more involved in the development of the soul and what we need for this development – and remember that this will involve some 'tough love' from time to time. If we keep an eye on the bigger picture, then effectively the tougher things are, then the more we can learn and the greater the progress we can make, spiritually.

Whatever we choose to call it, the concept of the guardian

Frank Capra • Yoav • Kelly Joe Phelps • Otis Redding

angel or personal daemon is a truly powerful one and an integral part of the human psyche.

Is it a good thing to have such a guide? Undoubtedly. If, as is suggested, we have within us a sort of personal counsellor who can, like Socrates' personal daemon, warn us clearly and concisely when we're doing the wrong thing, then what an incredible gift this must be.

There's often a deep divide between intellect and intuition, but I'm guessing we've all had those times where we've behaved quite irrationally for apparently no reason at all, and yet the reason has become manifestly clear at some point. Jackie is a no-nonsense medical sales rep working all across the south of the UK. Her story perfectly illustrates this dilemma, and thankfully, because she followed her intuition – which effectively amounts to the same thing as listening to her guardian angel – she was here to tell the tale.

Jackie's Story

'I don't know if the following is a story of angelic intervention or not. But the events that happened did possibly result in my being saved a very nasty incident.

'I was driving home from Bath one afternoon when I realised I had to fill up with petrol. Despite the fact that the fuel in my car was low, I went past one garage and drove on to the next. I filled up with petrol and thought to get a snack, but I didn't buy anything from the garage where I bought my petrol; I was at the checkout point with a sandwich and something made me put it back on the shelf. I got in the car and drove the 10 miles or so BACK to the first garage to buy something, and then found myself sitting down to eat a sandwich and drink some coffee despite the fact that I very rarely do that, and really needed to

The Buddha • *Otis Redding* • *Neil Young* • *Jeff Beck*

get home. This whole seemingly irrational escapade took me about an hour, and I was puzzled at my own strange behaviour.

'On the way home I passed a really nasty accident that had happened about an hour before I got there; a lorry had jack-knifed and was straddled across the lanes, three cars were involved in the crash. It was highly likely that, had I not taken that funny little detour, which had no rhyme or reason to it, that I was likely to have been one of the cars affected by the crash.

'Rationally, I don't really believe in the concept of guardian angels, not really. I am a very normal sort of person. But my behaviour on that day was really unusual, not 'me' at all, and I do wonder if I might have instincts that I never knew about. It's quite a humbling thought; that I obviously have something to do here that was worth someone, somewhere, saving my life for. It's made me ask a lot of questions, key amongst them being; am I in the right job? Shouldn't there be more to life than this?'

Jackie's subsequent questioning is typical of those who have had an angelic encounter.

Carlos Castenada · *David Attenborough* · *Brian Eno* · *Peter Gabriel*

20

Synchronicity

An Underlying Order to the Universe

T he next stop in our quest to pinpoint the nature of angelic energies is, for me, a particularly intriguing one.

Let's take a look at the series of events that sometimes occur in our lives which we call 'meaningful coincidences'. You know the sort of thing. You might be thinking of a friend that you haven't seen for years when you bump into them a day or so later. You could be in the middle of nowhere, even in a strange country, when you turn a corner and bump into someone you shared a house with during student days. A book falls open at exactly the page you were looking for. A parking space opens up for you in a crowded car park, just when you need it. Maybe you're shopping for something and the bill totals the exact amount of cash that you're carrying, down to the last penny.

You might choose to be sceptical and say that it's all down to selective perception and wishful thinking. It's almost impossible to measure, since the experience *is* quite a subjective one.

Carl Jung coined a term for these called these meaningful coincidences; he called them 'synchronicity'. He believed that synchronicitous events gave a hint about the underlying order of the cosmos, an indicator of the harmonious threads that tie all

Bob Geldof • *Bono* • *John Martyn* • *Chrissie Hynde*

things together. Further, he said that synchronicity was the 'acausal connecting principle' linking mind and matter, body and spirit, individual and the collective. Interestingly, recent discoveries in the new sciences (such as chaos theory and fractal geometry) are revealing to us that everything – people, animals, plants, molecules, cells, atoms, protons – are all participants in a huge, sensitive web of information.

If this is indeed the case, then we might want to suppose that synchronicitous events could be an indicator of those harmonious energies which can be called angelic.

My Story

I have a story of my own which is chock full of meaningful coincidences:

16 years ago, when I was heavily embroiled in the music business, I had to travel to west Wales to see a band that we were interested in signing. My husband Adam and I very nearly didn't go. Our usual car had broken down and it meant that we'd have to hire a car. It seemed that the only hire car left within reasonable distance of where we lived in London was a tiny little thing, uncomfortable and not really meant for long journeys. We took it anyway and had the most horrendous journey to Wales; Adam is pretty tall and was scrunched up very uncomfortably in the driving seat whilst I navigated, and although we travelled a very scenic route it took the best part of eight hours to make a journey which should have taken five. Suffice to say neither of us were in a particularly good mood when we finally arrived at a huge cattle shed on the Gwbert Peninsula, where the band were playing. To add to the tensions we arrived very late and caught only the last resounding chord of the last encore at a gig which had obviously been riotous!

Brancusi · George Best · Pele · Django Reinhardt · Sherpa Tensing

Someone lurched out of the crowd, saw Adam rolling cigarette, and asked for one; Adam handed over tobacco, pouch and lighter only to have the person disappear into the crowd. This incident further fuelled the hysteria...

We were booked into a B&B, so despite the setback of missing the band, we decided to make the most of the journey back, to amble and take time out to enjoy the countryside. Now, in my bag was a newspaper with houses for sale. The paper was called *In the Sticks* and is sadly no longer in print. It was basically the equivalent of a bin-end sale of houses and odd properties which were either unsellable or considered to be so. Desperate owners put their properties in this paper as a last resort, I think.

We'd flipped through this paper – which had been knocking around in my bag for a few months – over breakfast, because there was nothing else to read. One of the houses in the paper was not far off the route we'd planned to take heading home, so we thought we'd take a quick detour, purely to be nosy and because we had no particular plan about where to go.

Driving up to this house – which was tucked away down a lane, off several minor roads that got narrower and narrower and higher and higher up into the mountains – had a very strange feeling for both of us, of 'coming home'. This might sound fanciful, but it's true.

In any case, we couldn't get into the actual house since we hadn't bothered calling the estate agent, and the price on advert was too high for us to consider. But we pottered around, sat by the river, enjoying the sharp, acrid scent of the nettles heated by the scorching sun of a perfect late July day. We just couldn't shake off the feeling of coming home and decided that if we could stay the night with friends about 60 miles away, we should call and try to persuade the estate agent to open the house for us the next day – a Sunday.

Alexandra   David-Neal   •   Miles   Davis   •   David   Tomlinson

It was a very grumpy estate agent that met us at the house the next morning. Inside, the place was a mess; smelly, dirty, neglected, holes knocked in the walls and beer cans all over the place. But we were already sold. What's more, the house had been on the market for such a long time that the owners had dropped the price significantly just two days before. It was now exactly the price we could afford. But the estate agent was very off-putting. 'You'll never get a mortgage on a house in this condition', he said. 'And between you and me, the owner is a nutcase'.

He didn't explain why. He just seemed very jaded and depressed. But it really didn't matter! We had a very urgent feeling that we should live on that particular land — in many ways, the house itself wasn't by any means the main attraction. The landscape, however, needed no fixing up whatsoever. The estate agent seemed to be moving at a snail's pace and I eventually faxed over a letter so that they could send it on to the owner — this seemed to be the only way to get things moving. I waited anxiously for the phone to ring, which it did, a week or so after we had first seen the house.

'Well', said the owner, 'I've been messed around a lot with this house. If you're going to buy it I need the money by 7th August'. I was slightly nonplussed.

'Why 7th August?'

'It's my birthday', replied the eccentric owner.

'Good grief!' I said. 'That's my birthday, too!'

The owner didn't miss a beat. 'Well, this obviously means that you are the person that the house has been waiting for, but I still need the money by the same day'.

The next hurdle to get over was a bigger one. Would we be able to raise the cash in the short time available? On the morning that we were due to hear from the bank, I went out into the garden very early and found not one, not two, not three

David McAlmont · *Glenn Miller* · *Danny Kaye* · *Chi Fi Masters*

but no fewer than *nine* four-leafed clovers! So I knew that the bank would say yes and that we'd be able to buy the house.

15 years later I can tell you that this very precipitate decision, certainly the biggest impulse buy of our lives, turned out to be the very best thing we could have done and opened many doors and new avenues.

Now, all of this might seem pretty mundane. But there are factors which combined to make our purchase of this house, in which I am now sitting, possible:

The availability of a hire car and our determination to get to Wales despite the odds being stacked against us;
The proximity of the house to the route we took;
The change of price to what we could afford;
The fact that the vendor and I shared the same birthday;
The 'sign' of the nine four-leafed clovers.

This may all be very interesting, but what does it *mean*? Why should a series of coincidences have any great import? If you've been fortunate enough to experience this phenomenon, then you'll know that such a chain of events can have a massive impact on one's life. It's almost as though a line is being drawn around certain events with a cosmic highlighter pen, making you pay more attention than usual to linked events that seem to lead directly to a certain outcome.

Synchronicitous events are reminders of the underlying order of the universe, and tell us that angels are always at work. We may not always feel it or see it although it's always in operation; the magical times when its effects are obvious serve as a tantalising reminder.

Gustave Klimt • *Gustave Holst* • *Vaughan Williams* • *Stravinsky*

Lyndall's Story

'I had a weird one once. I have to start this story by telling you I'd been thinking for some days of a really good friend I hadn't seen for ages and had resolved to contact her soon. Anyway, I was at Earl's Court station; I'd been helping a blind chap when he got on the train and I'd also helped him off the train, my own train was coming in and if I helped him any more I was going to be late for what I considered at the time to be a make-or-break job interview. I had resigned myself to helping the man and ditching the interview when I spotted the friend I'd been thinking of, coming down the steps onto the platform. I told the old man to wait a moment, then ran up to my friend and, without any preamble, said "There you are! Can you take over looking after this blind man, please, I'm really in a hurry, I'll call you later!"

'My friend didn't bat an eyelid and took over acting as Sherpa.

'It was only later, when we spoke on the phone, that I realised what a weird, weird little event this was; me thinking of her, her being exactly in the right place at the right time after us not seeing each other her for two or three years, it all seeming perfectly normal at the time, and her immediate unthinking take-over. Weird. Oh, and I got the job!'

Lyndall's story touches the tip of the iceberg of those meaningful coincidences. It has been said that synchronicity acts as a sign that we are in the presence of angels/angelic energies. Why should this be? Well, to paraphrase Jung once again, he described these meaningful coincidences as both a reminder and an indicator of the underlying order of the universe; it appears to be within this state of order that angelic energies are most able to manifest to us. They're also a sign that we are on the

Beethoven • *Heinrich Biber* • *Rudolf Steiner* • *Paganini*

'right track', that we're doing the right thing; the purchase of the house, for example, might have seemed a bit stupid but all the signs were agreeing with our decision, reassuring us that we were making the correct decision.

Being open and receptive to synchronicitous events automatically means that we are living in the moment, free to follow leads and to unexpect the expected. This relates to being in the moment, in the Now, knowing that the universe will always give us exactly what we need, exactly when we need it.

Martyn's Story

It seems to be no coincidence that many of the people that came forward with stories of synchronicitous events have been involved in the arts or creativity. Such people are liable to think in a less linear way, they are more likely to take risks, and often they make sure – however subconsciously – that their lives are afforded a level of freedom to be able to follow their impulses. Martyn is a good example. He's a veteran of the music industry, responsible not only for writing several hits, but facilitating other musicians and writers to do the same.

'This story took place in 1989. I was having a rubbish time. I'd been living in Paris but split up with my girlfriend, whom I'd thought at the time was my "one and only". As well as feeling mentally and emotionally raw, to add insult to injury I'd kicked a wall in frustration and had broken my toe. So I was in a state of mental, emotional and physical pain.

'So I decided to move back to the UK, to stay at home for a while and lick my wounds.

'My Dad had a character working for him called Chris (you'll see that this name carries a great significance in this story).

Carlos Santana • *W B Yeats* • *William Blake* • *Ted Hughes*

Chris was an interesting bloke, and my Dad told me that he had said that he was a white witch. I didn't really even know what this meant, at the time. I do remember very distinctly that Chris gave me a penetrating look one night and simply said: "Don't worry...everything's going to be absolutely OK."

'The next day I got an unexpected phone call from friends back in Paris. They were offering me their flat to stay in for the summer, and use of their car; all I had to do in exchange was some tiling in their bathroom. So I went back to Paris the very next day.

'Back in Paris on my way to the flat, I dropped into a recording studio where I knew a couple of people. As I walked in, someone was holding the phone, asking if anyone could speak decent English.

'So I took the call. It was a girl called Christina, (that name again!) who was in a band that was pretty well known at that time, the DiVinyls. She was looking for someone to help set up their 8-track demo studio; I said yes, of course I'd go, and asked for their address.

'They were in a street called the Rue St Andre des Arts. I wasn't sure exactly where this was, so I borrowed a map book and hopped onto the Metro. I opened up the book and a business card fell out; the business card had on it the exact address of where I was headed for. Not just the same street, mind, but the same number and the same apartment!

'I arrived, met Christina and the band, and we got on really well. I spent a week helping them out and co-wrote the follow-up to the big hit they'd just had in the USA.

'Christina introduced me to a friend of hers, Christine. We fell in love pretty immediately, and I asked her if she'd ever seen the film *It's A Wonderful Life*. She hadn't, so I promised her that I'd take her to see it someday. A year later I found that the film was

Virginia Woolf • *Mo Mowlam Einstein* • *Debussy* • *Mozart*

showing at the Cinema Action Christine on the Rue Christine. Christine became my wife.

'We were together for a happy fifteen years, and my daughter, Angel, recently gave birth to my granddaughter – on Christmas Day!

'I certainly wouldn't describe myself as a Christian, by the way. The repetition of the name, Chris, Christina, Christine, and all the extraordinary "coincidences" at that time, acted as indicators that I was on the right track. They helped me recognise the beauty in all things, and the fact that we are all part of the underlying order of the universe'.

Instant Karma?

If we take the premise the meaningful coincidences can show evidence of the natural laws of a harmonic universe working themselves out, then it stands to reason that sometimes the conclusion of these forces may not be as good for one person as for the other. This particular story illustrates this point perfectly. Daniel is a high-ranking government officer working in south east England.

Daniel's Story

'I had a career crisis in 1996 after being unfairly sacked from a job at a transport consultancy who had hired me just in case they won a bid for a contract. They didn't win the contract and then sacked me. They also had a few criticisms (which I thought were very personal and not at all professional) to justify this sacking. Two men were behind this. Let's call them person A and person B. Person A carried out the sacking and asked me to leave the office, and told me I should speak to Person B about

Capability Brown • *Frank Lloyd Wright* • *Norman Foster*

the reason. I tried to contact person B but he avoided me and I was not given back my personal possessions. I also never received any kind of explanation for the sacking. I had only been there less than six months and had no employment rights. The whole incident was incredibly distressing, and to say I lost sleep over it would be a grave understatement.

'This sacking meant that I had to change career because word gets around in transport consultancy and I assumed I was finished, so, ever pragmatic, I trained to become a teacher which would have involved a much lower salary.

'A year later while doing this training and a bit of temping I found an advert for a well paying transport job in a local authority but my confidence was so dented I didn't see the point of applying. My flatmate persuaded me to apply and kept nagging me. I binned the application but he found it in the bin and insisted I apply even though the deadline had passed. I decided to apply, and then phoned the company to make sure it was still worth my while. They said that they had extended the deadline because there were not enough applicants. I went to the interview and got the job, based on them checking up on references.

'Unfortunately I had put Person A down as a referee, and after all my CV said I had worked for his company. I thought it unlikely that he'd give an accurate report. I was pondering on how to deal with this as I was waiting at an underground station when all of a sudden I spotted Person B. He had seen me and edged away so I literally chased him up the platform and jumped into his carriage as the doors were closing. I said: "How are you? I need to speak to you. Will you give me a reference?"

He was rather afraid and embarrassed and felt he had to say yes, so I got the reference. Throughout all this I didn't ask him about the reasons for the sacking or his elaborate avoidance of

Joan of Arc • *Jimmy Page* • *Jimi Hendrix* • *Robert Plant*

me. In the end he asked me to write the actual reference, presumably so that if there was a problem he wouldn't be blamed, but one year into the job I discovered the company had been happy to give me the job based on the strength of the interview alone, and that the reference had been a formality. My career then resumed and I was doing better than I otherwise would have.

'This is not the end though. The whole story starts to get very odd. Three years later I was in another job with the government and I had to hire a transport consultant to work on a contract I was managing. As chance would have it, Person A's firm bid for the job, with Person B on the list of contractors. Person A's firm did not get the contract because they had put in the bid incorrectly – this process can be incredibly bureaucratic, and in this particular world, form matters. I need to say also that the decision was not in my hands; I wasn't in such a powerful position at that time. However, Person A then told our Head of Procurement (who was on the decision-making board) that I had a grudge against him and his firm because he had sacked me in 1996. He also suggested that I had lied on my CV. Fortunately I was well established by then and nobody wanted to listen to him, so the Head of Procurement invited him to a meeting to discuss it, and invited me to come in about ten minutes into the meeting. He had not told Person A that I was invited and Person A looked appalled and terrified when he saw me. The Head of Procurement then asked him to repeat his allegation to my face and Person A imploded. The Head of Procurement then said he would stop his company getting any government contracts if he questioned the judgement of a government officer again (i.e. me). I was then given the task of showing him the door.

'I later discovered that the whole 1996 debacle had been Person B's idea. Person B wasn't very nice and had worked

Josh Homme • *Kurt Cobain* • *David Bowie* • *Frank Sinatra*

abroad. He boasted that he had eaten whale meat in Japan and said he saw nothing wrong with it. I once saw him in a pub bolting a hot dog down his throat and it reminded me of an article I'd read in the independent suggesting that these caused cancer of the oesophagus especially if the person was already obese.

'Well, about a year later I went to the offices of Person A's company to discuss a contract they had been given. The meeting was held in the room I had been sacked in. I saw a very thin man with baggy skin on his face like a deflated balloon. It was just recognisable as Person B and he looked very sorry for himself; I asked a colleague if that was Person B and he said yes. I said he seemed to have lost weight and the colleague said, yes he's had cancer of the oesophagus. Weird. Even weirder, Person B died three weeks later.

'It felt to me as though I was simply the catalyst in the whole event, that the subsequent misfortune that happened to Person B wasn't anything to do with me; if there is such a thing as angelic forces working via the means of instant karma, then ultimately he brought his fate upon himself'.

Bach • Carole King • W.M. Turner • Dali • Stubbs

21

Speaking of Meaningful Coincidences

What about the feathers issue?

It's always been something of a curiosity, for me, that there is a prevalent belief that where a white feather lands, an angel has been lurking. All the 'big' angelologists seem to hold this almost as a tenet of their faith. Surely it makes more sense to view the feather as the presence of a creature a little closer to home – i.e. a bird? The fact that it is a bird that drops the feather, rather than an angel, is after all no less of a message or a reminder from divine forces. Since time immemorial, all races, all cultures, looked to the skies and to the movements and flight patterns of birds (called auguries) to deduce the whims and wishes and actions of the Gods. It is for this reason that birds are closely associated, symbolically, with angels, and so feathers have gained a powerful resonance too, because of the same associations with transcendence and being able to operate in another dimension.

Bunuel   •   *Terry Gilliam*   •   *Degas*   •   *Diaghilev*

However, the 'feather thing' is really too prevalent to dismiss easily. If we take the feather not as a physical piece of evidence as to the presence of an angel, but as a symbol of the Angelic, then it starts to make more sense. The following story, from Antoinette Lawrence, is fairly typical. Antoinette is an author, Reiki master and healer, specialising in flower essence remedies. Antoinette is also a psychic, so a real all-rounder!

'I was ironing my husband's shirts in the kitchen at the new house and, being in a slightly tetchy mood because things didn't seem to be going my way, said out loud that angels never seemed to be around anymore and that they obviously didn't want to hang around this particular house. However, when I took the shirt off the ironing board there was a small white feather! Not a huge thing in itself, but a reminder that we mustn't take anything for granted. I was rather surprised and said a quick apology for having had any doubt.'

Antoinette occasionally reads angel cards for people, and the following incident took place during just such a reading.

'The next occasion was with a friend. She is a reiki master and a very wonderful person, and I was giving her a reading from my Angel cards. We both saw a ghost walk past the dining room window (we witnessed the same thing – a lady in white in an old-fashioned dress) and I said, in a very cocky way: "Well, there might be ghosts all over the place but your guardian angel doesn't seem to be here right now!"

'But then we both noticed, at the same time, a single white feather on my friend's sleeve! It's fair to say we were both a bit staggered after this 'double whammy' encounter with first a ghost and then an angel...

Leonardo Da Vinci • *Oscar Van Gelden* • *Chris Heywood* • *Galileo*

'I have to tell you, I've never been cocky since that day!'

Here's another story of an interesting journey that came about because the participants decided to be 'led' by feathers. The story comes courtesy of Sandra Cooper.

'In 2007 a friend and I decided to set ourselves a personal challenge by walking from Southport to Hornsea, some 224 miles. Both of us are 50+ and I am certainly no seasoned walker so this really was something of a crazy challenge, but naiveté and innocence are often the best allies when it comes to carrying out daft ideas!

'We set off on August 18. As we set off on the walk the heavens opened and we were utterly soaked for the whole of the first day. We also got lost due in no small part to locals having fun with the signage, and our B&B, although really very pleasant in many ways, didn't afford us the best of experiences.

'On the 19th we started out with another very wet day of walking, joined by a friend who lived across in the west of England and the route today was from Alderhay to Wigan. Although it was still pouring down, the new company was inspiring, and although my friend and I had been on the verge of giving in and going back home, we decided to carry on and just give in to circumstances, to "go with the flow".

'After about 20 miles we stood on the side of the canal with two possible paths ahead of us and there was no way of knowing which one led to our chosen destination. Neither was signposted. We really didn't want to run the risk of extending what was turning out to be a wet, cold, sodden and miserable journey. As we stood at the junction two dogs appeared from the path to our right. One was a huge great black Great Dane and the other a Golden Retriever. We decided to wait for their

Fra Angelico • *Alexander Graham Bell* • *Stravinsky* • *Magellan*

owners, so we could ask them with was the best path to take to the warm, dry, friendly hostelry that had tempted us in the guide book. But after a good 5 minutes of waiting no-one had appeared. The dogs seemed to be waiting, so we decided that we might as well walk with them along the same path. They kept on walking ahead of us as though they were guiding us. They would play for a bit, then wait for us to catch up. We followed the dogs for two or three miles and found that they had effectively brought us to exactly the place we wanted to be, but were no-where to be seen and the owners of the pub had no idea about them; who they belonged to or where they lived.

'This whole incident was so odd that we decided that we would just trust our instincts and, if lost, we jokingly said that we would look for white feathers since we'd heard that they were meant to be signs from the angels. The next morning we confidently went on our way.

'The third night found us at the home of a man who had previously been a Buddhist monk. We found him, believe it or not, by following what seemed to be a trail of feathers. I wouldn't have believed it if it hadn't happened to me. This man was compassionate and delightful and he saw us on our way on the morning of the 21st. Thank goodness, by now the rain had stopped and the morning was bright and sunny, the day was sparkling as though freshly-minted. That evening we found another wonderful place to stay, with a woman who had lost her nineteen-year old son in the army, and who had developed a beautiful peace garden. How did we find her? There was a white feather on top of her hedge...

'The entire walk took us 11 days in all. It was a remarkable opportunity to really follow our instincts and to trust in the signs that we had chosen to follow, rather than slavishly follow maps.'

Newton • Pythagoras • Boudicca • Plato • Aristotle

The telling thing about Sandra's story was her conscious decision to 'let go' of all the conventional ways of setting about such a long journey, and to rely instead on 'signs' in the form of dogs, and then the feathers. By noticing the small signs around them, they accessed the synchronicitous events that put us in harmony with the universe. Take note that this 'letting go', surrendering to being in the moment, is a key factor in allowing angelic energies to enter into our lives.

This final story is from Vanessa, whose powerful experiences resulted in her running her own angel workshops.

'Some years ago, I was locked into a very abusive relationship, which I knew, for my own health and sanity, that I needed to get out of. But with a small baby and no job, and no money of my own, I really couldn't see a way out.

'This might sound corny, but this was all about the time that Robbie Williams's song 'Angels' was being played absolutely everywhere. At the same time, I watched Diana Cooper on TV talking about angels... and suddenly I was very aware of angels. There were angel statues, angel books... you name it, I noticed it. I had read in a book that a white feather was a sign that the angels were near. I prayed and prayed for a white feather or a sign to confirm the existence of angels. After two months of praying I was sitting in my front room with my baby, was singing to her. I had never felt such love in my life as the love I had for my child. As I sang, I saw a flash of light in the corner of the room. I gently put my daughter down and walked over to where I had seen the flash of light, and as I walked to the corner a white feather fell before my eyes, slowly and peacefully. It was a magical moment, and from that day on my life changed completely. I prayed for guidance on my relationship and one night at about 3am, a blue light appeared beside my bed. It was

Socrates • Mary Magdalen • Blessed Virgin Mary • Brunel

pulsating and I knew everything was going to be ok. I felt very strongly that this was Archangel Michael.

'Not long afterwards I had the strength to end the relationship, and I started doing aromatherapy treatments from home. In 2000 I organised a Mind, Body and Spirit festival. I knew it was something I had to do and everything ran really smoothly, although I had never done anything like this ever before. I easily got plenty of exhibitors, I had Native American performers at the show, I had performances and workshops all day and I have to say, I was very proud of myself for finding the wherewithal to arrange all this — as anyone who is a single mum will know, juggling things isn't always easy. A couple of days after the show I was in bed with my daughter and we were talking, then I saw a quick flash of blue light at the bottom of my bed. My little girl was three or four at the time, and I asked her if she'd seen anything. "Yes", she said. "That looked like the man who was at the show". I asked her, what man? She replied: "The one who was dancing, with all the feathers".

'This was the first instance that my daughter showed of being in contact with the unseen worlds. During the time of my daughter being aged three to eight she saw so many things that she amazed me.

'I would just like to tell you one more story. My daughter was about five and we were staying with my Mum. We were sleeping together in the same bed, and one evening there were in the room what I can only describe as lots and lots of small golden dots moving around. We held our hands up and played with these dots. I could see that one was on the tip of my finger and my daughter said "Look at that gold dust on the tip of your finger!" To me it was confirmation that we were experiencing something very special together.

'The realisation that there are angels in my life changed

Marie Curie • Louis Pasteur • Hypatia • Oracle of Delphi

things forever. From being a person with no direction, I finally found a direction and a purpose in my life. I always question what I see and I am a very practical, logical person, but what I have experienced since that day of the flash of white light and the feather, has been incredible. In fact, I must just tell you one more thing...when I had a stall at a mind body spirit festival selling my oils I was next to a lady who organised workshops etc. The business she had was called "Soul Journey". I took a risk, and told her that I could organise Angel Days and workshops, and she gave me a booking for four months' time. Although I was petrified about what I had let myself in for, had never actually done any kind of a workshop and had no experience of speaking in front of people, it went incredibly well, and I manifested my dream of working in some capacity to spread the news about angels. I now run my own Healing School, and my life has completely transformed.'

Sir Christopher Wren • *Laurence Olivier* • *Bronwyn Bunt* • *Dante*

22

Orbs

A relatively new phenomenon, orbs appear only in digital photographs, not on film; these transparent floating balls are believed by many to be a manifestation of angelic energies. Others believe that they are the work of the Devil; another school of thought holds the more pragmatic point of view, that they are merely dust motes either in the air or in the lens of the camera. The small golden dots described by Vanessa sound very like orbs.

Either way, the study of orbs is taking up a lot of time right now, with such luminaries as Diana Cooper, one of the world's leading experts on all things angelic, being one of the most illustrious advocates of the 'orbs as angels' theory. As well as angels, Diana says that orbs can be fairies, spirit guides, elementals, which each have individual purposes, for healing, enlightenment, or to help us attune to certain energies. Again, the phenomenon is something that's very easy to be sceptical about and, as usual, you can find the scientific theory that matches your own.

The whole 'orbs' phenomenon was recently given a further boost when TV star Noel Edmonds became and an advocate for their spiritual potency in an interview with the *Daily Express*. More usually known for TV shows such as *Deal or No Deal* or the popular Saturday kids' TV series *Swapshop*, Edmonds believes

Lynne Lauren • *Chrissie G* • *Adam Fuest* • *Jack White*

that he has a ball of shimmering light that glows over each of his shoulders, casting a protective aura around him at all times. Noel equates these orbs to the spirits of his dead parents who continue to take care of him from the otherworld.

'I have two orbs that visit me,' Noel says. 'They're both the size of a melon and one sits on my arm and the other is over my shoulder. I like to think they're my parents. Conventional photography can't pick them up but digital cameras can. My belief is that these are something to do with some form of spiritual energy. And possibly because I miss my parents like mad, I like to think they are them.'

In many ways, speaking out like this in public is a courageous move for Noel and has caused sceptics to look askance. But it's probably safe to say that unless he was convinced about these 'angels' then it's unlikely that such a public figure would open himself to ridicule.

Noel Edmonds believes that these little balls are in fact the essence of energies either angelic, or left behind by a deceased human being. Edmunds equates orbs with positive energy. 'It's inconceivable to me that when we die, that energy just disappears. That energy has to go somewhere. That's what orbs are. I'm absolutely certain now that there is something else out there because I've got the proof.'

The interesting thing about orbs isn't really whether they 'exist' or not. Whether they are dust motes or evidence of angels is somehow arbitrary; what matters is that, for some, they are proof of divine energies, revealed to us via the modern technology of digital cameras. Many of our most profound spiritual experiences are incredibly personal; ('you had to be there!') and listening to other peoples' stories often requires a suspension of disbelief especially if we have not experienced a similar event that would provide a frame of reference.

Lisa Johnson • *Sarah Gregory* • *Einstein* • *Tania Ahsan*

INTERMISSION

By way of a brief interlude before we tackle Part Two, which shows you exactly *how* to access and harness the angelic energies that we've been investigating, I know that you will enjoy this incident from the life of Jamieson Wolf, which, although true, is written in the style of a short story.

Life is Magic
by Jamieson Wolf

I remember how cold the air was.

January had hit with a vengeance and the snow was crisp and cold. It was minus thirty degrees Celsius and I was bundled into my hat and my thick wool scarf. I was none too happy about the cold.

Actually, I was none too happy about anything at that moment.

Life, it seemed, did not want to go well for me at that point. I was in the middle of an abusive relationship, I was miserable at my job and I was quickly falling into a downward spiral.

Rather than do anything about the job or the relationship, I was instead living in deep denial about my unhappiness and masking my feelings with large doses of weed, cigarettes and booze.

Mark Townsend · Florence Nightingale · Roald Dahl · Ernst Haas

I had cut myself off from my family and friends and chose to live in my misery, thinking that no one could see it, that I was putting on a good front. If I thought I was fooling others, I was wrong. I was only fooling myself.

That day the cold seemed to bite at my exposed skin as I lit a cigarette and waited for the bus that never seemed to come on time. I had finished my shift at work and it had been another horrible day of micromanagement, angry customers and yelling people. I worked at a call centre answering questions about billing and technical issues. I hated every moment of it.

If I'm going to be honest with myself, I hated every aspect of my life at that point. I was, in fact, contemplating suicide. I thought it would be easy, so incredibly easy, to take a bunch of pills and not wake up again. I thought of how the pills and booze would momentarily warm my insides that seemed to match the coldness that was around me.

I stood there, waiting for the bus, cigarette smouldering away and I was thoroughly depressed with myself and with my life. I prayed that something would change, that something would give, so that I could find myself again.

It was then that I saw the black man.

It was not uncommon for strangers to approach me at bus stops and ask for change or for cigarettes. I geared myself up for my usual response (*No, this is my last cigarette* or *No, I don't have any spare change*) as the man came closer to me. But what came out of his mouth was not a demand for money or tobacco.

It was something else all together.

'Are you Palestinian?'

'What?' I said. I was sure that I had misheard.

'Are you Palestinian?' the man repeated.

'No.'

'I thought you might be, 'cause of the way you have your scarf.'

Ansel Adams • Simone Johnson • Alan Card • Mike H • Judika Illes

His voice was low and seemed to rumble out of him. I caught a whiff of booze coming from him and wondered if he was drunk.

I reached up and touched my wool scarf. It was a light blue mixed with white and it was bundled around my neck so that it billowed out of my coat. I felt like a large turtle, but I was warm.

'Nope. Sorry,' I said.

'I saw you walking from far away. I thought to myself, that guy is either Palestinian or Jewish. You Jewish?'

'Nope.'

I wished for the man to go away. All I wanted to do at that moment was to smoke my cigarette and indulge in my pity party. I had had a long day and I was tired and all I had to look forward to was going home to someone who didn't love me, no matter how much I loved him. I didn't want to talk to this man, didn't want to listen to him. He didn't seem to care what I wanted though.

'You gay?' the man asked.

I drew in a shocked breath and didn't answer. I didn't think it was any of the man's business.

'You gay?' the man asked again.

'No.' I said.

'Then why you got those ear rings?' the man asked. 'That means you're gay, don't it?'

I turned and looked at him for the first time. He was black, skin so dark it was the colour of night. He was dressed well, but looked like he had seen better days. And he reeked of alcohol.

'What's it to you?' I said defensively.

'So you do have a tongue in your head. I wasn't sure you did, you know? So you're gay, right? Those gloves, they're rainbow coloured.'

I looked down at my gloves. They were striped in purples and blues, but far from the rainbow of colours used to identify gays

All the contributors to this book • *James Lebon* • *Joni Mitchell*

and lesbians. 'They're not rainbow coloured. They're just gloves, is all.'

'Just gloves?' replied the man. 'But they keep your hands warm don't they? If they do, then they's magic gloves, wonder dust gloves. Who give you them gloves?'

'My mother.'

'And do you think of your Ma every time you put them on?'

'Yeah, I do, actually.'

'Then they's magic gloves, my friend. I know you gay guy, even though you won't tell me. But I want you to know that I'm okay with that, I'm cool with that. Some guys, my friends, they kick your ass from here to there, but me, I'm cool with that, good with that. You understand?'

'Sure.' I was beginning to get a little uncomfortable around the man. There was something in his eyes, dark and deep, that told me the man was not all there. His eyes looked as if his sanity was straddling both worlds: the mundane and the beyond.

'Good. Let me tell you something, you listenin'?'

'Yes, sir.'

'Good, now listen. 'Cause I'm not going to say it but once, alright?'

'Alright.'

'Here it is: everything in the world is magic. That there is the most important piece of information that you'll ever hear. Everything in the world is magic. Say it.'

'Everything in the world is magic.' The words felt funny coming out of my mouth, as if my tongue was thick. The fear increased slightly but, strangely, I didn't feel as if I was in any danger.

The man nodded at me, the light from a streetlamp making his eyes seem glassy. 'But only we can make the magic. The magic is inside of you, do you know that?' He took a step towards me. 'Only we can control the magic.'

Rhona Heath • Bobby Osborne • The Penponties • Lewis Carroll

I took a step back from him, feeling the fear rise up inside of me. 'I don't understand what you mean.' I told him.

'Everything in life is ours, with the magic. You have only to take control of your life to see the magic work, you see?'

I shook my head, speechless.

'You have to take control of your life. Now, I know you're gay, but you don't have anything to worry about from me. My friends, they'd do you some terrible harm, but not me. I'm telling you, everything in life is magic. You have to make your own choices, better choices, for the magic to come.'

I heard the rumble of the bus as it came closer to me. Part of me was filled with relief that the bus was here; but part of me was also filled with a sadness. I knew that I would never see this man again. I couldn't explain this emotion.

He looked at the approaching bus. 'That your ride?' he said, motioning with his head.

I nodded.

'Well, you get on it and get on home. You think about what I told you.'

I nodded again and got on the bus. When I had taken my seat, I looked out the window to see if he was still there, watching me. There was no one there.

Later that night, after another fight with my boyfriend, with new bruises on my body, I was sitting in the washroom. In front of me was a glass of water and a bottle of pills. I was woozy from too much pot and my throat hurt from too many cigarettes.

I stared at the bottle of pills. I knew that if I took them, I would not wake. I wondered what it would be like to have an eternal, dreamless sleep.

But in my pot-induced haze, something came back to me. I remembered what the black man had said at the bus stop:

'You have to take control of your life. Now, I know you're gay, but you

Zoroaster • John Dee • Nancy Palmer-Jones • Adam Fuest

don't have anything to worry about from me. My friends, they'd do you
some terrible harm, but not me. I'm telling you, everything in life is magic.
You have to make your own choices, better choices, for the magic to come.'

I stared at the bottle of pills and knew that they were the
wrong choice. If I took them and embraced that never-ending
sleep, it would solve nothing.

I put them back into the medicine cabinet and drank the glass
of water. I was thirsty all of a sudden. Thirsty for what, though,
I was not sure.

I grabbed a cigarette from my pack on the coffee table in the
living room. My boyfriend ignored me and that was fine with me.
I went downstairs, lit my cigarette and sat outside on the front
porch of my house. I listened to the night noises around me.

'You have to make your own choices.' I whispered. 'Life
is magic.'

I knew that I would have to do two things. I would have to
end my relationship with my abusive boyfriend. And I would
have to quit my job. I wasn't sure when I would be able to do
this; it could be now or later, but I knew it would come. The
decision had been made.

I sat there in the darkness, the immensity of the decision like
a punch to the gut. I took another drag of my cigarette and
stubbed it out. I took one last look at the darkness, the lights
playing in the shadow. I had never realized how magical the
world around me really was. But I had been too blind, or too
depressed, to see it.

I knew that breaking off my relationship and quitting my job
was only the beginning. I knew that getting my life right again,
crawling out of the downward spiral I had let myself spin into,
would take a long time.

But, with time, I would heal.

I opened the door to go inside, but took one last look at the

Jeanne McKenzie • *Robert Atherton* • *Doreen Virtue* • *Jacqui Newcombe*

shadows. I watched as a white feather floated down from the sky, somewhere above me, and landed right at my feet. I picked it up and it felt soft in my hand. I looked around for a bird, but saw none. I knew that the feather did not come from a bird.

It had come from him. I'd like to think that he was telling me to spread my wings, to let myself fly. I put the feather in my pocket and looked one last time at the darkness. 'Thank you.' I said.

I went inside and gathered what strength I had to face what was to come.

Diana Cooper • *The Prophet* • *Roald Dahl* • *Paulo Coelho*

PART TWO

ACCESSING AND HARNESSING
YOUR OWN ANGELIC POWERS

*'I just talk to them in my head. Sometimes I see them but
mainly I talk to them in my head. It's not hard to do. They tell
me things sometimes and sometimes they show me things that I
wouldn't have seen, like when they told me to look down in
the long grass and I saw a dragonfly being born'.*

—MILLIE, AGED 7

So, we have seen how angels have appeared to us in art,
ancient and modern.

We've looked at ancient texts, examined religious beliefs,
and heard remarkable stories of first-hand encounters and
experiences of angels from credible and realistic people.

We've seen how artificial intoxicants can allow us to enter
the realms where angels dwell, and how angels can appear in
guises and forms that are not necessarily what we would expect.

It's easy to see lots of this evidence as purely circumstantial,
but the fact that angelic forms have been a part of our lives for
millennia, and the sheer weight of circumstantial evidence
would point towards the fact that yes, creatures such as angels

Jesus Christ • *Jeremy Clarkson* • *Patti Smith* • *Tim Smit*

and the angelic energies certainly do exist. This is despite the fact that we can't apply empirical standards to them, we can't weigh or measure them.

Let's play devil's advocate, though, and address a couple of tricky questions before we go any further.

Anita Roddick • *Alexandra David-Neal* • *Dalai Lama*

23

Do I have to Believe in Angels to Access Their Energies?

OK, in a book called *The Magic of Angels,* such a question might seem to be a contradiction in terms. Also, the fact that you're reading this would imply at the very least a curiosity about the matter of angels. But it's not always easy to believe in something that, as we've seen, is very much a matter of deeply personal experience.

But it's not, and no, you don't necessarily have to believe wholeheartedly in angels in order to access their energies. You do, however, need to suspend disbelief and remain open-minded. But then, you wouldn't be reading this if you didn't know that already. I'll say again; an open mind is the only requirement. That, and a healthy dose of common sense. This whole area is prone to fantasy and wishful thinking which unfortunately can cloud the issue. There are enough bizarre and

Barack Obama • *Jules Verne* • *Frances Drake* • *Dylan Thomas*

173

outlandish stories out there to cast doubt on those experiences which are clearly full of honesty and integrity, so it's important to keep a level head when dealing with metaphysics.

There's a great line in Paulo Coelho's book *The Valkyries*. The book tells the story of a man's epic search for his own guardian angel. 'He knew, though, that whether one believed in them or not, they were always there – messengers of life, of death, of hell, and of paradise'.

If you can accept that there may be discoveries yet to be made in our universe, then we can assume that you are a sane and rational person. After all, the power of electricity existed before we knew how it worked or how to harness it, and before we even gave it a name. We have a degree of control over electricity but many aspects of it remain elusive; our endeavours to catch lightning have succeeded to a certain extent but there's a random element that remains beyond our grasp and which can wreak havoc from time to time.

Discoveries in the fields of modern physics and what are termed the New Sciences are going some way towards explaining many of the hitherto inexplicable aspects of the Universe.

A few centuries ago, people with the power to heal might well have been hounded out of their villages and burned to death at the stake. And yet today there are practitioners of, and courses for, reiki healing, energy healing, chakra healing and similar the length and breadth of any high street. The proliferation of such treatments must mean that they are efficacious – mustn't it? And yet the way the practitioners work would appear to the casual observer to be incredible. The laying on of hands is a skill which has been practised since time immemorial and continues to have a beneficial effect; we still cannot explain absolutely precisely, exactly and with certainty, how it works.

Robbie Burns • T.S. Eliot • Jeremy Sandford • Bruce Chatwin

24

Do I Need to Believe in God to Access Angelic Powers?

No. You don't.

No ifs and buts; you really don't need to believe in any kind of a higher power to believe in, or to experience, angelic energies.

You'll see that during the course of this book I often seem to be using this language guardedly, since I don't want to rule out any possibilities in actually interpreting what these energies really are. The term 'angelic' seems to be as good as any although I am aware that this might be off-putting for some people.

Although our latter-day ideas about angels are laced with biblical imagery, the idea that angels are messengers of a god or gods is overlaid into the original meaning. Bear in mind that the word angel means 'messenger'; there's no original mention of any god, although this interpretation is often assumed. Again, it

Beryl Nozedar • *Trevor Nozedar* • *Andrew Catlin* • *Edith Piaf*

all comes down to definitions. Even if you believe in a god or gods, your interpretation might be very different from the person sitting next to you. It might be that you subscribe to the theory that God is a man with a beard sitting in a throne in the sky. On the other hand, your 'God' might be a very personal interpretation of universal creative energies that are divorced from any idea of man having been made in an image of anything at all. Frankly, this is the explanation that I find the most comfortable and most universally acceptable and non-exclusive.

It's a fact that the angels that we encounter in the Bible or the Qur'an have provenance prior to the written word; we can see as much in very early examples of prehistoric art, as mentioned earlier in this book. We've seen how different societies and cultures have, at different times, overlaid the ideas and identities of these 'angels' with their own interpretations, and we, naturally, continue to do the same thing.

In other words, if this isn't too much of a contradiction in terms, we have to both embrace all the archetypical ideas that we have about angels at the same time as throwing them all away. After all, a cliché is a cliché exactly because it is so meaningful! Now, more than at any other time in the past, we need to look at everything to do with angels – and demons, for that matter – in a completely different light.

Billie Holiday • *James Watt* • *Louis Armstrong* • *The Searys*

25

Who's In the Room?

An Angel for Every Eventuality

The further you delve into angelic lore and history, the more you start to realise that, as well as the hierarchical divisions, there seems to be an angel for everything.

There are several ingenious books on the market that contain extensive lists of the labyrinthine correspondences between angels and their roles. These books list angels for every eventuality and tell us which angel presides over what, from archery to zoology including janitors, telephones and laptops along the way.

Now, there are differing schools of thought about whether you need to contact specific angels for specific jobs. It could be argued that such supernatural beings may not operate under the rules that we have for ourselves – after all, it's strange to think about there being a sort of bureaucratic system of angels. It's also possible that we are not always the best arbiters of what we need in our lives and so wouldn't necessarily know which angel to consult; best leave it up to them. There's yet another

Theo   Chalmers   •   Janet   Gleghorn   •   Edmund   Hilary

argument that says that angels, by their very nature, don't need specific roles.

On the other hand, it seems reasonable to suppose that if we're going to make a plea for something specific, it would only be polite to make sure that we are appealing to the correct entity. However, the issue is complex and the angelic correspondences differ sometimes between sources. The hierarchical system that we investigated earlier in this book only adds further to the confusion.

I also sometimes wonder whether we might be imposing human conditions on non-human entities? Are we so keen on making lists, categories, catalogues and indices that sometimes we can't see the wood for the trees? We already know that we can't weigh or measure angels, and that they certainly won't stay put in any boxes that we try to fit them into. What's more, we know that they are the ultimate shape-shifters!

If you really want to attach an angel to your specific request or situation, then there are numerous sources which will enable you to find out exactly who is who and what is what. I would suggest a different approach, though, a much simpler, fuss-free one. When you're contacting your angels, simply ask for a name rather than imposing one. If you have been given a name that you don't recognise, I would recommend Gustav Davison's *Dictionary of Angels* as being one of the most comprehensive and informative catalogues in the field. It's especially interesting when you're given a name that you really don't recognise. Of course, it's possible that you might have heard these names before and not paid much attention, when the word might have become lodged in your subconscious. But it's equally possible that, by remaining open to possibilities, we are more able to allow the angelic energies to flow in a more natural way that isn't restricted by our own expectations and set of rules.

Douglas Bader · Elvis · Grace Darling · Rosa Parks

The Big Three

That said, there are three key angels that are common currency amongst not only experts, but lay people. During the course of researching this book, these three appeared more often than any others. These angels, whom everyone has heard of and who have pretty much attained superstar status, are Michael, Gabriel, and Raphael.

The information that we have about these beings comes not only from the Bible and those parts of the Bible that are generally omitted, such as the Book of Tobit, but also from art, literature, poetry and also perceived belief, those ideas that seemingly emerge from no one particular source but which have an important part to play in our collective visions, notions and memories.

Let's see what each of them are all about, and let's also see just how complex our beliefs are even about these three very famous angels. Since lots of other people have encountered these angels in person, there's reason to suppose that you might too, so I've included a quick snapshot of each of them. Incidentally, I've listed them here in alphabetical order rather than trying to imply any sort of hierarchy between them.

GABRIEL
Identifying Features:

Linen Robe
Trumpet
600 wings (or, in the Qur'an, 140 pairs)

Famously known as the messenger who breaks the news to Mary that she's going to have a child, the role of this angel is a crucial one in school nativity plays. However, it's not only the birth of Christ that Gabriel predicted; he also foretold the birth of John the Baptist.

Christian Barnard • Simon Clayton • Esti Clayton • Linda and Dominic

Big not only in the Judeo-Christian tradition but in Islam, too, where he's known as Jibril, Gabriel is one of only two angels (apart from Michael) who is actually mentioned in the generally-accepted version of the Old Testament (which omits the Book of Tobit).

Gabriel's first appearance in the Bible, though, comes in the Book of Daniel. Gabriel appears to tell Daniel the meaning of the visions he's been having, which relate to the 'end of days'.

The role of Gabriel is a varied one, with what appear to be some of the strange discrepancies not uncommon amongst angelic types.

Gabriel is the angel of resurrection and death, mercy and vengeance, revelation and annunciation. Mohammedan belief describes Gabriel as the spirit of truth that has having 140 pairs of wings, and who dictated the Qur'an to Mohammed. Cabalists identify Gabriel as being dressed in white linen, a description that appears in Ezekiel Chapter 9.

...Another of the many legends about Gabriel concerns the days of the Nephilim, the giant half human, half angel hybrids. Gabriel was sent to set them fighting against themselves so that they would effectively kill each other and therefore solve the problem of what to do with them.

It's a commonly-held belief that Gabriel will use his distinctive trumpet to signal the End of Times and the resurrection. This belief stems not from any biblical source but from Milton's epic poem, *Paradise Lost,* a good example of popular culture informing an idea. Here, Gabriel appears as the chief of all the angelic guard in paradise.

This is a good example of how relatively recent art and literature can inform our collective ideas of angels. Longfellow's *The Golden Legend*, too, has a powerful and lyrical

Marco Polo · *Alex Maiolo* · *Stanley Meyer* · *Nikola Tesla*

contribution to make: Gabriel appears as the Angel of the Moon, bound to bring hope to all of mankind.

Latterly, there have been varying interpretations of Gabriel. For example, in the movie *Constantine*, Tilda Swinton plays an intriguingly androgynous Gabriel who teams up with the son of the Devil. In a similar devilish twist in *The Prophecy* trilogy of films, Christopher Walken's Gabriel is jealous of human beings, and after railing against God he is given the opportunity to experience life as a normal man for a while. Eventually Gabriel is reconciled with Heaven and given another chance to revert to his proper angelic form.

MICHAEL
Identifying Features:

Sword, shield and helmet
Armour or a breastplate
Warrior-like pose and countenance
Often seen standing over a dragon, which represents the Devil.
Sometimes has a set of scales in his hands.

Known as the 'field commander of the army of God', it's appropriate that one of Michael's most distinctive features is the sword that he holds aloft and the warrior-like breastplate that he's often depicted wearing.

In the Old Testament Book of Daniel, Michael is identified as the protector of Israel, another reason why he might need that sword. Michael is also described as the Prince of Light who leads the forces of God against the 'Sons of Darkness', the evil forces lead by the demonic God, Belial. In Daniel's vision, both Gabriel and Michael fight together to vanquish the angel Dobiel. Michael's soldierly aspect means that despite his origins as an archangel, he has been rendered into a saint, and as St Michael he is the patron of warriors and soldiers of every sort

Lynne Lauren · *Tylluan Penry* · *Bill Gates* · *Warren Buffett*

— hence the proliferation of chivalric orders that bear his name.

Much of what we know about Michael from any ancient writings stems from the Book of Enoch.

Michael, like Gabriel, has some anomalies, but is perhaps more clearly defined. He is the angel of mercy and forbearance, described as patient, merciful, and an escort of God.

It was Michael who, legend has it, kept an eye open for mankind when Adam and Eve were ejected from the Garden of Eden, was the first to bow down before a human being, and also kindly taught Adam the secrets of agriculture. There's also some speculation that it was Michael that gave instruction to Moses on Mount Sinai, and also handed him the tablets of the law. It's said that it was Michael, too, who appeared to Moses once again in the incident of the Burning Bush.

Like Gabriel, Michael has a handy knack of interpreting visions for people. Notable amongst these is Enoch's vision. Michael tells Enoch that his vision means that for those who obey God, the Day of Judgment will be a joyous occasion, whereas for sinners it will be a day of inquisition, when all the evil spirits that have been supported by human flesh will actually bear witness against the people that hosted them.

Kabbalists believe that Michael is the chief defender of the Jewish peoples, and in particular he defends Israel from a supernatural enemy that appears in the form of an angel called Samael.

Although Jewish laws effectively prohibit angelic intervention between man and god, believing instead that prayers should be delivered directly to Head Office, as it were, Michael's position as a petitioner to God on behalf of mankind means that he does occupy a place in specific prayers, although it's probably true to say that these prayers are no longer as popular as they once were.

It's also written in the Book of Daniel that, in the 'end times',

Prof Alan Jones • Phillip Carr-Gomm • Stephanie Carr-Gomm

it will be Michael who eventually triumphs over the Antichrist. Whereas Gabriel will sound the trumpet, it's Michael who will hold open the gates of Heaven for the righteous to gain entry.

There's a Christian legend that says Michael often appears in scriptures although his actual name isn't mentioned.

Despite his war-like countenance, the early Catholic Church accorded Michael with the care of the sick, and this tradition might well be why many latter-day healers cite Michael as a source of angelic aid. There are many, many holy and sacred springs all over the world with perceived healing powers that are attributed to Michael, and there was once a major sanctuary about 50 miles outside Constantinople that bore his name.

The River Nile was placed under the protection of Michael by the early Egyptian Catholics, and today we can spot places that have come under the influence of this great angel quite easily, by examining names; Mont St Michel in Normandy, for example, named since Michael is also the patron and protector of sailors. St Michael's Mount, off the Cornish coast, is named for the same reasons.

As Christianity took hold of Europe and the rest of the world, many of the old Gods were superseded by characters from the new faith. Consequently, the reason that so many mountainous places, and chapel and shrines at altitude are named for Michael is because he took the place of the Old Norse god Wotan, the former ruler of mountainous places.

The scales that Michael sometimes holds are because, as the Angel of Death, he is accorded the job of carrying souls in those scales up to Heaven to be weighed. In this same guise as Angel of Death, it was Michael who told Mary when she was about to die.

Michael also has a profound role to play in magickal and hermetic traditions. Here, he is identified as coming from the South, carrying the element of fire with him.

Yuri Gagarin • *Buddy Holly* • *Ennio Morricone*

RAPHAEL
Identifying Features:

Often carries a vessel of some kind
Sometimes accompanied by a young man – Tobias
Often carries a staff, or a fish
Appears as a handsome young man.

There's a modesty and humanity about Raphael which is very appealing. Indeed, Milton describes him as 'a sociable angel' in his epic poem *Paradise Lost*.

Raphael appears in the Book of Tobit, which is omitted from the conventional form of the Bible. Although he is not mentioned in the Qur'an and never mentioned in the accepted version of the Bible, this angel has really grabbed he collective imagination and also has a powerful role to pay in the people's lives.

Raphael's name means something along the lines of 'God Heals', and so it's no surprise that this angel is a favourite amongst the latter day healers who call upon angelic energies in their work. Such is Raphael's influence in the area of healing, that the Hebrew word for a doctor is '*rophe*', a word directly derived from Raphael. It was Raphael who handed Noah the reassuringly practical gift of a medical volume once he was restored to solid ground after the flood.

Raphael is often depicted with a young boy, Tobit, as in the book of the same name Raphael, disguised as Azarias, protects the young man along his journey from Media to Nineveh, dealing with demons and healing Tobit's father's blindness along the way, amongst other feats. Raphael also releases Sarah from the evil hold of the demon Asmodeus who is responsible for the trail of dead husbands left in the poor woman's wake. Why Raphael is sometimes depicted holding a fish? It's because he uses the gallbladder of a fish caught by Tobit to heal his father's

David Lynch • *Amy Johnson* • *Donald Campbell* • *Amelia Earhart*

eyes. The same fish is used to drive away the demon Asmodeus, who departs when the liver and heart of the fish are burned.

Raphael only reveals his true identity to Tobit at the very end of the journey, when he says that he is 'one of the seven holy angels' that are attendant on the actual throne of God.

Unlike Michael, who is honoured in the names of many places all over the world, Raphael has far fewer places named for him. Despite this, and the fact that he doesn't appear in either in the Bible or the Qur'an, Raphael is a profoundly important angel. He is said to be the Angel of the Sun, the guardian of the West and the governor of the South.

Raphael is said to be one of the seven angels of the apocalypse and also, curiously, a guide in Hell; another role which we wouldn't normally associate with an angel.

There's a nice piece of lore about Raphael, too, concerning Solomon's building of the first great temple at Jerusalem. Solomon prayed to God for assistance in the building, and was answered in the form of Raphael, who came bearing a ring upon which was engraved a five-pointed star known as the *pentalpha*. This symbol fortunately had the power to calm and subdue any lurking demons; handy, given that the actual temple was legendarily built with the slave labour of demons that were subdued by Solomon, presumably using his magickal ring.

The Next Big Four Angels

Traditionally, angels seem to appear in groups of seven. A few examples? There are seven angels who rule over the 196 provinces of Heaven. There are seven angels in the Yezidic belief, an interesting and controversial offshoot of Islam which has been (incorrectly) aligned to devil worship. There are seven angels of punishment.

John Morris • *Ron Edwards* • *David Lynch* • *Henry Miller*

There are also seven angels that rule over the days of the week, and the seven planets of the ancient world. The names of these angels do vary according to which source you are reading, and it's a good assumption that the spellings of these names vary, too. To add to the confusion, some angels also appear as demons.

In any case, it seems the right thing to follow in this great tradition and mention four other key angels for the purposes of identification.

URIEL
Identifying Features:

A fiery sword
Can be depicted coming from heaven in a chariot
drawn by four white horses
As St Uriel, has a symbol of an open hand with a flame
Has sometimes appeared as a burning serpent

Uriel is an interesting angel, generally grouped with the Archangels, and is said to have brought to mankind not only the secrets of alchemy, but also the Cabbala (although it took intervention from another angel, Metatron, to give us the means to understanding it). It's Uriel who stood at the gates of Eden with his flaming sword, barring return by Adam and Eve. He's also the angel of repentance, and was the one of the angels credited with warning Noah of the impending flood.

SANDALPHON
Identifying Features:

Very, very tall.
Appears in sandals when in the presence of God.

Sandalphon is the twin of Metatron, one of the great angelic princes and master of heavenly song. He's incredibly, unbelievably tall; one description says that he 'exceeds

Doug and Joy • *Ellen Macarthur* • *Jont* • *Oppenheimer*

Hadraniel [in height] by a 500-year journey on foot'. That's tall! Moses, too, called him the 'tall angel' and Sandalphon's head apparently reaches as high as heaven itself. Sandalphon gathers up prayers, making garlands of them, which he then sends to heaven in the shape an orb. Sandalphon also has an unceasing war with the forces of darkness as personified by Satan.

Sandalphon's name gives a further clue about his appearance, in that he wears sandals whenever he appears before God. One of his more unusual attributes is that he can influence the sex of an unborn child.

METRATRON
Identifying Features:

Very, very tall
36 pairs of wings
Innumerable Eyes

Although he doesn't seem to figure very largely with latter day angel therapists, etc, Metatron is one of the most powerful angels of all, so much so that he has been referred to as 'the King of all the Angels'. You can read more about the relationship between Metatron and Carlos Santana elsewhere in this book. Like his angelic twin Sandalphon, great height is one of his attributes. In fact Metatron isn't only tall, but huge; his size is described in the Talmud, as 'equal to the breadth of the whole world'. Metatron is described as the link between the human and divine worlds, is the angel that records everything and as such is the heavenly scribe (and for this reason is sometimes identified with Hermes/Mercury). Gabriel and Sammael are Metatron's subordinates to whom he gives orders regarding the souls that will be taken at certain times; as such, he is the supreme angel of death.

Freud • Jung • You • Picasso • Lyn and Margaret Regan

ARIEL
Identifying Features:

The name of Ariel means 'Lion of God' and so
he often appears with the head of a lion.

Ariel is the name not only of an angel but of a demon, a city, a man, and an altar. Sometimes the name is used as a substitute for the holy city of Jerusalem. Raphael, the great healing angel, is sometimes assisted by Ariel. The controller of demons, Ariel also rules the winds.

If this short 'how to' guide whets your appetite for angelic identification, there are umpteen books on the market which will give you far-ranging and concise descriptions of the many, many angels and demons that you might encounter. Bear in mind, though, that in making contact with your own angels, it's not necessary to get bogged down in all this detail unless you really want to.

Me • Ptolemy • JK Rowling • JRR Tolkien

26

The Ultimate Shapeshifters

Angels in Disguise

'...They can take whatever forms a person imagines they have.
Because they are God's thoughts in live form, and they need to
adapt to our wisdom and knowledge. They know that if they
don't, we'll be unable to see them'

—The Valkyries, PAULO COELHO

Although we're now very familiar with the archetypal angelic
forms, it makes sense that, if we are going to be party to
aid from angels, then they wouldn't want to frighten us out of
our wits or cause undue distress; heart attacks from shock
appearances of a heavenly host would after all be
counterproductive. We've seen how Angels traditionally present
themselves. It's also necessary to take on board the idea that
angels can, and do, appear to us in disguise. These creatures are
the ultimate shapeshifters, it seems, so be prepared for any and
every eventuality!

In putting together this book several stories have appeared in
which the angelic energy has appeared as a harmless old

Pablo Casals • Jaqueline DuPrey • Maria Callas • Carl Sagan

eccentric, the sort of person that we see every day but don't pay an awful lot of attention to. That is, until we have interaction with them.

The following anecdote comes courtesy of Terry Green, drummer with the band 'Shabby Rogue'.

Terry's Story

'I was feeling at what was probably my lowest point back in St. Helens many years ago. Nothing seemed to be going right for me. I felt as if I'd had enough of everything. Also, I was involved in some rather horrible things that I'd really rather not talk about; druggie stuff, to be honest with you.

'Anyway, one day I was walking down the street, not really knowing where I was going and just thinking black horrid things when suddenly this eccentric old guy that people called 'Johnny Wellies' on account that he always wore wellies (how imaginative!) appeared at the side of me, walking along next to me. Obviously, I was so wrapped up in my own dark cloud that I wasn't aware of him straight away, but then realised this presence alongside me. I'd never actually spoken to him before.

'I remember him asking if I was OK. I said no, I wasn't OK, in quite a dismissive way. But he took no notice of my rudeness, just walked alongside of me all the way down the street and talked to me, in a kindly way. I can't really remember exactly what he said but it was really uplifting and by the end of the street I felt like I'd come out of a black hole.

'Johnny Wellies then calmly said "ta-ra" to me and toddled off in a different direction.

'Now, I'm not necessarily saying that this old tramp was an angel, but him walking along with me like that, and just being kind and saying these uplifting things was exactly what I needed

Jonathan Cainer • Dame Margot Fonteyn • Nureyev • The Heathies Ghandi

at the time, although I certainly wouldn't have gone looking for it; I'm not the type to seek out counsellors and people like that. I kind of felt he knew what to say to me, right at that moment, and I've never gone back into such a black place.'

The following story is from Anita, who works in music PR in London.

'A few years back, I was having a dreadful time. I found out my long-term boyfriend, to whom I was engaged, was having an affair; not only that, but he'd got the 'other woman' pregnant. Add to the equation that she was someone that I was also doing publicity for and had considered to be a friend; you might start to understand the depth of my despair. He was begging her to have an abortion and begging me to stay with him but I just wanted to disappear into a black hole and not have to deal with *any* of them anymore.

'I was living near Portobello at the time and often used to see an old bag lady collecting bits of rubbish, especially at the end of market days when lots of the traders leave behind fruit and vegetable trays if the produce is coming up to its sell-by date; I guess lots of homeless people get to eat like this. Anyway, I ended up just sitting down in a doorway, and watching the business of the world on my doorstep that I'd never really bothered to notice before. I was miserable as sin.

'Then I saw the old bag lady walking towards me. She was looking at me and walking directly towards me. She was rummaging about in her pocket. She came and sat down next to me and pulled out from her pocket a perfect, red, shiny apple. She took hold of the bottom of my coat and started polishing the apple, looking down apologetically at her own dirty clothes. Then she handed me the apple with a big, bright smile. I started to cry;

•   *Stephen   Hawking   •   Mother   Teresa   •   Peter   Sellers*

still without saying anything she put her arm around me and I laid my head on her shoulder and just bawled and sobbed like a baby. All the time she just stroked my hair and held my hand.

'The odd thing was that everyone just went about their business as though we were invisible. Maybe we *were* invisible?

'I'm not sure how long I sat there but eventually stopped crying, and wiped my eyes on a bit of old rag that the bag lady handed me.

'Then we both went off our separate ways. I can't tell you whether this lovely old tramp lady was an angel, but the gesture of bringing the apple, and sitting with me whilst I vented all this grief, and her silence, is one of the most profoundly strange and comforting things that have ever happened to me.'

The following is another account of a possible angel in disguise. It comes from Karin, a fine artist living in Wales.

'This maybe isn't a paranormal experience or a serious comment, but I thought I'd pass it on anyway as its rather poignant and may ring bells with other people. My dad has dementia. When he was at a fairly early stage of the disease he was admitted to hospital with a kidney infection. During one visit he kept saying he could see an angel. In the bed opposite was a very old lady with quite a lot of fluffy white hair, so perhaps my dad was confused. However, I like to think that he saw her as an angel and indeed wonder if she was. His dementia is Lewy body disease and the early stage is characterised by hallucinations but I often wonder whether the disease had released a usually-inaccessible part of the brain thus enabling him to see what he would previously have dismissed.'

The concept of an individual angel that helps out with fairly mundane things is relatively well accepted. When you think about it, angelic intervention for such unimportant matters is highly incongruous. Then again, it's often these small reminders that speak most eloquently of the unseen world. Actually, it seems that appearance of such supernatural help isn't that unusual; during the course of my research I found that there were several instances, for example, of 'parking angels' who seemed to be leading the fortunate driver to a convenient parking space. In fact, on a recent Radio 4 documentary, Gloria Hunniford mentioned that very phenomenon.

The next anecdote comes from Bronwyn, and describes the appearance and actions of her very own 'travel angel'.

'My "travel angel" always appears to me in the same form. Having travelled a lot over the last couple of decades, all over the world, I have found myself hopelessly lost on many occasions. At first it just seemed like a lovely coincidence, but after so many repeated sightings I would just look for him when I needed him. You see, my "travel angel" is a grey-haired man who wears a cap and a neutral-coloured tartan jacket, carries a tall walking stick, has a dog and wears no socks with his wing-tipped shoes. I'm not making this up. So on one of my adventures Netty, my sister-in-law and close friend, was with me and we were taking our kids (who were all quite young at the time – both my boy and girl were young enough at that time to still be in nappies) for a weekend in Carmarthen. We had our route all mapped out, planning to take main roads only, until the kids reached that point where they couldn't take it anymore. They needed to eat, drink, run, scream – we were on the edge of a serious freak-out, so we pulled off the main road in search of food. We were in Wales, so of course we were soon very, very lost. Luckily we saw a series of signs for a pub so followed those (blindly) until we

Richard Burton • *Finlay, Janette and Tyler* • *George Harrison*

found it. Now we really don't know where we are or what direction we would need to go in to find the main road – and the pub is closed. Children still freaking out, I looked at Netty and told her not to worry because our man with the dog would come and help. We got the kids out of the car so they could at least have a stretch and Netty wanted to know when our man would turn up because we were stuck. I swear, at that moment a gate opened in the hedge bordering the car park and he stepped through with his dog. He walked right up to us and asked if we needed help. I explained that we had come off the main road in search of food and now were very lost. He said we didn't want to eat at the closed pub anyway because they didn't cater for vegetarians (I did *not* mention that I was a vegetarian.) He then proceeded to give us directions back to the main road that would have us into town and parked at the vegetarian restaurant within ten minutes. Netty was speechless. We needed him, I told her he would show up, he always shows up and he did.'

Jeremy Clarkson: Unexpected Angel?

With due respect to Jeremy Clarkson, it's true to say that angelic energies are not necessarily the first thing that you'd think of when describing him. Jeremy is a highly-intelligent, funny forthright journalist, and he'd probably be the first to agree that 'angelic energies' wouldn't readily be associated with him. Nevertheless, it seems that there might be more to him than meets the eye. How so? Read this story from Nerys.

'I live in quite a mountainous part of Scotland. I can take a shortcut to work by driving over a particularly steep mountain pass; this knocks about seven miles off the alternative journey which effectively takes me around the hilly bits.

Terry Gilliam • *David Lean* • *Michelangelo* • *Jim Morrison*

'One January day two years ago I was in a hurry, and though it was icy and snowy I decided to risk the shortcut. After all, I had taken the same route before in bad weather and have a four-wheel drive car.

'On this occasion, however, the road was really bad. The mountain pass in particular doesn't get sunlight until quite late in the day, if at all during the winter, and the ground was covered in frozen ice with a layer of slippery fresh snow on top of it.

'As I reached the summit of the hill, despite the fact that I was in four wheel drive and going very slowly, the car started to skid very badly on the ice. The left-had side of the road is a sheer drop, and it's this that I was heading for. I was just about to go into complete panic road when I heard, as clear as a bell, that slightly hectoring voice of Jeremy Clarkson in my head. He said, "Don't apply the brakes. Take your hands off the wheel. The car is designed to right itself".

'This was so unutterably weird that I did as I was told; and sure enough, after twirling about a couple of times, the car really *did* right itself, and ended up facing the direction I needed to go in.

'I carried on calmly down the hill, but when I got to the bottom it really got to me; the full force of the danger that I'd been in, and the sheer bizarreness of being advised out of what could have been a really nasty accident by the disembodied voice of Jeremy Clarkson. I mean, of all people! This isn't something that happens every day, and I had a stiff whisky when I got home that night! Is it possible that Jeremy Clarkson is in league with angels?'

Frank Capra • *Yoav* • *Kelly Joe Phelps* • *Otis Redding*

27

How to Meet an Angel

Now it's time to apply some of this information.

Before we go any further, though, I should say that although we'll be looking at harnessing your own angelic powers, I have ruled invocations out of the equation. This is a huge area and there are many texts available on the matter, written by experts. Invocation is a complex subject and for me, attempting to command any spirits, let alone angelic ones, is a matter left well alone.

I'd even go so far as to say it's quite an impertinent thing to try to do. No-one likes being told what to do, especially not supernatural beings. Even so-called experts have got into a sticky mess.

In any case, making contact with your angels should be a simpler matter than following the labyrinthine articles of a fully-fledged invocation.

The most important thing to acknowledge, above all else, is this:

THEY ARE ALREADY HERE.

Start to look at your life in a different way, focus on all the unexpected little things that seem to beam in from nowhere to solve problems or make you feel better.

The Buddha • *Otis Redding* • *Neil Young* • *Jeff Beck*

The very first step in finding these powers is to acknowledge something that is within you; that is, your intention. Keep your intention pure. Ask sincerely that your angelic powers will make themselves known to you.

Focused Intention

Prayer, meditation, spell casting: all are forms of focused intention which enable us to clarify our aims and make their realisation more likely. Sometimes it helps to have a physical manifestation of this intention, and you might want to emulate this ancient tradition – which transcends barriers of all nearly all faiths, religions, and spiritual practises – by constructing an altar and placing upon it some key symbolic tools.

Carlos Castenada · *David Attenborough* · *Brian Eno* · *Peter Gabriel*

28

Magic for Angels
Creating a Sacred Space

Do you have a quiet corner somewhere in your house where you can create a place to help you focus your intentions? It doesn't need to be massive, and also doesn't need to be particularly noticeable if you don't want it to be. Preferably it should be somewhere where you can be private; perhaps in your bedroom.

Effectively, what we're going to make is an altar. In doing so, we will be following a very ancient idea. Let's look at the reasoning behind the altar, and the ritual items that are placed upon it.

Altared States – the meaning of the altar

In ancient times, mankind worshipped high places, such as the sky full of stars at night or sunshine during the day, and also, by association, mountains, because these high pieces of land were closest to the heavens. There are innumerable mountains of sacred stature all over the world, and it's notable that messages from the Gods have historically come from mountainous areas – Moses' tablets of the Law are a good example.

Bob Geldof • Bono • John Martyn • Chrissie Hynde

The word 'altar' actually means 'high place', and by worshipping at an altar we are acknowledging a primal instinct to honour a high place.

Creating an altar in your home is a lovely thing to do, and if you have the space, it's good to leave it intact. Another basic instinct means that we face the direction of the rising sun, but this actually isn't utterly essential. Maybe you have an inspiring view that will serve as a wonderful backdrop.

The actual altar itself could be something as simple as a window ledge, or you might want to make something fancier. It's entirely up to you.

Brancusi • George Best • Pele • Django Reinhardt • Sherpa Tensing

29

Ritual Items

To be absolutely honest, you don't really need any of the following items at all: if you're in the right state of mind you can simply close your eyes, let go, and talk, like Millie, whose quote I used at the beginning of this section of the book.

However, it's not always possible to regain the simplicity and purity of mind that a child can access so easily, and sometimes we need help. The following implements have been in use for thousands of years in rituals and ceremonies, no matter what they are or what tradition they come from. Scratch the surface and we're all the same, we have the same ideas about what works, ways of expressing externally the workings of the inner mind. These items are as much for us as for the entities were attempting to contact. After all, this book is full of stories about angels that have come unbidden and unannounced with no ceremony whatsoever.

Bells

In the film *It's a Wonderful Life*, Clarence the Angel explains to Jimmy Stewart's protagonist George Bailey that every time you hear a bell, 'an angel gets its wings'. Now, at the risk of sounding

Alexandra David-Neal • *Miles Davis* • *David Tomlinson*

ditsy as hell, there's something to be said for that, and it's no accident that the bell is an important ritual item in many religions. The sound of a bell – or a Tibetan bowl – not only calls the spirits to us, but sends them away; the sound of its chime calls our attention to the 'here and now', and as any good musician knows – let alone a sound therapist – the mood and intention of the person doing the playing is instantly communicated, on a higher level, wordlessly. The vibration of the sound exists on many planes and is a reminder of the unseen world. The naked eye cannot 'see' sound without special apparatus – we can only see the effects of it. And yet it exists and is powerful enough to move things physically by the waves of its vibration; think of story of the Walls of Jericho!

Incense

Another reminder of the unseen world, the scent of incense is another stalwart of spiritual ritual. The heady aroma can have transportive powers and assails the senses with a very accessible and clearly defined form of beauty. And symbolically speaking, the sight of smoke spiralling upwards has been a sign of communication with the Heavens from the peace-pipe of Native Americans to the fragrant frankincense that's burned in censers by the Roman Catholic Church. If you've never experimented with incense, don't go for the ultra cheap stuff. Invest in some charcoal tablets and good quality grain incense, such as frankincense. If this isn't readily available, get some good-quality Himalayan or Indian stick incense.

Candles

Or flame, of any description. Candles tend to be the most convenient way of getting fire safely and controllably into any

David McAlmont • *Glenn Miller* • *Danny Kaye* • *Chi Fi Masters*

environment. The alchemical symbol for flame is a triangle that points upwards towards the sky, a reminder of the 'as above' that is the Heavens, the direction from which, traditionally, angels arrive. The presence of flame brings the male element to your altar.

The colour of the candle is key, too, although a plain white church candle will do very well. Use your instincts and select what appeals: no need to go delving through colour charts. We all know instinctively enough what certain colours are for and what effects they have upon us.

Chalice

Effectively, the shape of a chalice, or bowl, represents the inverted triangle that is not only the alchemical symbol for water, but the sign used to define the feminine. This inverted triangle represents the female sexual area, lyrically known as the Delta of Venus. The chalice should hold some water in it, neatly bringing the female element to your altar.

Flowers

Spirits like flowers. Who doesn't? Doesn't need to be a huge bouquet, just a single bloom will do, or even a sprig of herbs.

The prettiest offerings I've ever seen are the little ones that are set out every morning in certain parts of Bali, generally where roads or routes cross. These are just a simple little dish, with a leaf, some incense, a piece of fruit, a single bloom, and a sprinkle of water. So you see that your altar doesn't need to be complex. In fact, in many ways, the simpler the better, each component added with meaning and intention rather than creating a jumble of extraneous 'stuff' - but it does help to know the elements of a

Gustave Klimt • *Gustave Holst* • *Vaughan Williams* • *Stravinsky*

timeless tradition, a tradition that really does transcend racial and political boundaries, that you are also a part of.

Statuary

Some people like to have a statue as the main focus of their altar. Rather than having anything too specific, you might want to think about using something which symbolises the idea of an angel. A feather immediately springs to mind. Not only is a white feather a popularly-perceived angelic symbol, but the feather itself stands for flight, transcendence, and the higher realms. Make sure that the feather has been 'gifted' to you, i.e. found, rather than plucked or from any contaminated source.

Beethoven • *Heinrich Biber* • *Rudolf Steiner* • *Paganini*

30

Meeting Your Angels Halfway

So, now you have a space which will provide a focus for the work you're going to embark upon with angels. What comes next?

We need to take a close look at how our own mental attitude affects everything around us – including our capacity to recognise the angelic energies that surround us.

The Power of Positive Thinking

The way we choose to look at things is fundamentally important to the experience we have of life. Here's an example.

Recently I met a lady who came to me to ask if I could recommend a lucky charm or a spell; she was going through a very bad patch, she said. She seemed to be quite down and depressed, so I asked her if she minded telling me what sort of bad luck she was having.

'Well…my dog was run over and became very very ill and had to have a series of operations which cost just over a thousand pounds. It was awful'.

Assuming that the dog was dead, I commiserated, saying how

Carlos Santana • *W B Yeats* • *William Blake* • *Ted Hughes*

awful it was to lose a pet. 'Oh no', she said. 'He's not dead. He's absolutely fine, but it cost a lot of money'. I was nonplussed. I asked her if she'd rather have a live, healthy dog and a huge vet's bill, or a dead dog and money in the bank.

'Oh, of course I'd rather have the dog!' she said, looking at me in disbelief.

I suggested that this was a choice that she'd been able to make; that in fact this wasn't an incident of bad luck, but the contrary. She hummed and hawed and then reluctantly agreed.

'That's not all, though' she said. 'We have a holiday home on Anglesey and the boiler needs to be replaced. That's more expense'.

Again, I was utterly bemused. The person who was with me, listening to all this, started to laugh.

'So', I said, 'let me get this right. You have a healthy, happy, alive dog. You have a second home on Anglesey. And you're telling me you're unlucky?'

The look on the woman's face was classic. Then the truth dawned on her, and she started to laugh as she realised just how lucky she was. She'd got stuck in the consideration about the money; this was getting in the way of the truth.

I guess we all have moments like this in our lives, when we can't see the wood for the trees. It's important to shake ourselves out of this from time to time, however we might choose to do it. I agree, we can't all be Pollyanna all the time but given the choice, how would you choose to think —positively, or negatively?

Making Choices

What is all this to do with accessing angelic energies, whether we believe in them or not? The point is that if we allow for the

Virginia Woolf • *Mo Mowlam* • *Einstein* • *Debussy* • *Mozart*

possibility that we can see things in a different way – however unreasonable it might seem – then we open ourselves up to all sorts of possibilities. If we remain closed – i.e. if we think negatively – then many delightful things remain inaccessible to us. The idea here is to get back to that child-like state of anticipation and excitement, when the world really was full of infinite possibilities. The possibilities are still there – it's our minds and attitudes that change and sometimes become jaded with the passage of time and sheer world-weariness! Again, I'll go back to what I said in the introduction to this book; we have a choice, every single time. It's what sets us apart from the beasts. Never allow yourself to forget this.

Capability Brown • *Frank Lloyd Wright* • *Norman Foster*

31

Cosmic Ordering versus the 'Gratitude Attitude'

Cosmic Ordering is big business right now, promulgated by all sorts of celebrities. It's not surprising really; the idea that the Universe is ours and that we can wish for whatever we like is an attractive one and it's tempting to run up a sort of Christmas list of stuff that we believe will make us more fulfilled, more successful, more satisfied with life, richer, happier, more beautiful. It's also an interesting phenomenon since it was recently proven that if we write things down, then they are 25% more likely to happen. There are all sorts of reasons for why this might be but the primary one is that, by thinking about what we actually want, we focus our thoughts and so make the efforts needed to make whatever it is more attainable. It's easy to drift through life doing the same old stuff with no thought about the bigger picture.

Here's a thought, though. What if we already wished for all those things? What if we *do* actually live in the best of all possible worlds, every waking moment of every day, only we can't

Joan of Arc • *Jimmy Page* • *Jimi Hendrix* • *Robert Plant*

always see the woods for the trees? Be careful what you wish for...here's a salutary tale from Amanda.

'About two years ago I was really broke – I'd lost my job and I was having real problems finding one that would pay me enough money to provide decent childcare for my children, let alone anything else. Looking back on it, things weren't *that* bad; I just hated being on benefits.

'Anyway, one evening a friend came over and we did that Cosmic Ordering thing where you write down what you want on a piece of paper and then burn it. All I wrote was that I wanted lots of money within three months.

'The horrible thing, and the scary thing, was that I got the money, but only because of the sudden death of my father. It sorted me out financially but the way it came to me was horrific. I wish I'd just asked for a new job.'

Amanda's story is terrible but we can learn some lessons from it, and the first lesson is to learn just how powerful we can be. Sometimes when we truly realise this it's tempting to just run away and hide from it. This is one of the reasons why people take refuge in addictions such as drink, drugs, gambling, shopping. They're distractions; sometimes they're *nice* distractions, but that's inevitably what they are. True realisation of our own power can be scary, and it brings with it a great responsibility.

The second is to be careful what you ask for. Amanda got what she wanted, but not in a way that was pleasant or easy. She also realised that the thing that she had asked for was not in fact the thing that she really needed. Be careful when asking for material things; specify exactly what it is you really want. Do you want money, or the security that it can bring you? Do you want a relationship, or do you want friends and company to take

Josh Homme • *Kurt Cobain* • *David Bowie* • *Frank Sinatra*

you away from a lonely life? Do you really want a well-paid new job, or do you want to be respected more for what you are doing and perhaps offered a promotion?

Cosmic ordering is an interesting phenomenon when it comes to the realisation of angelic powers. There's a way of reconciling your life which is much easier than making long lists of stuff — that is, to accept that we already ordered everything that we have.

There's a simple exercise that you can do which really DOES help you to connect with the angelic powers that we all have access to. In a way, it turns the idea of cosmic ordering on its head as you realise that you do in fact have absolutely everything that you need. The thing about cosmic ordering that I have never felt entirely comfortable with is that it makes you concentrate your thoughts into the areas of wanting things; there are always going to be more things that you want and fewer things that you actually need to make your feel complete and fulfilled. It's quite a big difference in approach.

The Gratitude Attitude

You won't need much for this exercise — just a piece of paper and a pen.

Start to write down all the good things about your life. They don't need to be big, flashy things. Start with the small things that we often take for granted. Start off each sentence with the words 'I'm grateful...'

For example:

I'm grateful that I'm healthy

Bach • *Carole King* • *W.M. Turner* • *Dali* • *Stubbs*

I'm grateful that I have a roof over my head.
I'm grateful that I have enough to eat.
I'm grateful that I live in a comfortable climate
I'm grateful that I have clothes to keep me warm

And so on. You could even start with:
   'I'm grateful to be alive, right now, in this body, on this planet, at this time'.

Next, take all the things that you are unhappy with in your life, one by one. Don't write them down; just hold each thought, one at a time. As you do so, see the positive side of the situation. Here's an example. Your negative thought might be that you are unhappy in your job. Instead of dwelling on this idea, write down 'Job'. And then write down the positive aspects that come with it; for example:

I'm grateful to be earning money.
I can walk away at 5pm and don't have to think about it until the next morning, so I am free!
The people I work with are nice.
It is a stepping stone to my true vocation.

And so on.

You will find that, by applying positive energies to all the things in your life that you are unhappy with, not only your mindset but the actual situation itself will start to turn around. Don't be afraid to look into the nooks and crannies of your life to root out every single aspect that you're unhappy about. We already know what incredibly powerful beings we are – now is the time to start applying this power.

Bunuel   •   *Terry Gilliam*   •   *Degas*   •   *Diaghilev*

As we've mentioned, it isn't always possible to be some kind of Pollyanna-type person all the time. On the other hand, given the choice of putting a little effort into positivity reaps way greater rewards than the time you'll spend doing so.

Next, take all these positive aspects of your life that you've written down and cut them into strips and put in a box. Every morning, first thing, take one of these things at random and just read it out loud; no need to do anything more elaborate. You will probably find that there are many, many other ideas that you can add to your box of good things to consider.

Leonardo Da Vinci • *Oscar Van Gelden* • *Chris Heywood* • *Galileo*

32

Are You Ready to Receive?

What has this got to do with accessing angelic powers? Well, it helps to put you in a receptive frame of mind. Also, rather than simply asking for things, this simple exercise helps you to focus on just how much positivity you have in your life. Keep the exercise going for as long as you can and you may well find that the list of things that you thought you needed to complete your life may well not be as long as you thought. Have you ever been annoyed by a demanding child at a party who never seems satisfied, but always demands more of this, that or the other? Angelic energies react favourably to an already-positive thought pattern; they are attracted to it.

Ever had a friend that always seems to have things going wrong in their life? Whatever happens, it's a disaster? These might be little things (such as a car breaking down or losing a key) but these people can make such a huge fuss that the 'disaster' is all out of proportion. On the other hand, you may have another friend who seems genuinely to have difficulties, but always puts on a cheery face and is much more pleasant to be around than a person who is always complaining and moaning.

Like attracts like. Angelic energies – positive, vibrant forces

Fra Angelico • *Alexander Graham Bell* • *Stravinsky* • *Magellan*

for good — will be attracted to the same sort of energies that you choose to put into the universe. Thinking positively, seeing the good in everything, not only makes your own life more pleasant but sets up a similarly positive vibration in the universe which will actively enhance and promulgate your positive experiences.

Don't worry, I know it's not possible to be positive *all* the time, and some days you just want to blow a raspberry at the world. I've done it myself. But the main thing is that you are aware that you are making a choice, and that you have the freedom to do so. Depression is a terrible illness, and often remains undiagnosed. If you are prone to depression then it's a good idea to seek medical advice or to try effective remedies such as St John's Wort. Depression, despite being a common affliction, is not a natural state of mind and it's a mistake to take it for granted or to think that it's just 'one of those things'. In many ways, depression can be a sort of luxury, often the affliction of the modern age when we don't know what it means to have a difficult life.

Good luck engenders good luck, but it's all a matter of attitude. If we think we're lucky, if we believe we're lucky, then good things continue to happen to us. Like the lady with the healthy dog and the holiday home who thought she was beleaguered and couldn't see just how fortunate she was, it's all a matter of how you think of things.

Which would you choose?

Newton • *Pythagoras* • *Boudicca* • *Plato* • *Aristotle*

33

Forward Projection

S o, now we know that we can affect our lives and the lives of those around us by choosing a simple shift in attitude. Let's take this a step further.

Imagine that, consciously or not, you chose every single aspect of your life as it is today. Yes, that means everything – even the problems, the seeming failures, and the tragedies. Whether this is actually the case or not doesn't matter – what's crucial in this mode of looking at things is that by taking this attitude we allow ourselves to accept responsibility and see things in a different way.

So, then, how about if it's possible to project forward, to imagine where your life might be five or ten years hence? To be able to see the bigger picture without worrying too much about the issues that face us right now, all those day-to-day things that loom large but are forgotten about a week later? To help you to do this, think back to the last time your world seemed like it was falling apart. It might have been a death, a failed relationship, redundancy. And yet you're still here. Chances are, things are better than you could have possibly imagined they could ever be. Think of how you felt back then, in the middle of

Socrates • Mary Magdalen • Blessed Virgin Mary • Brunel

the maelstrom of emotions and anguish, and then see what benefits were rendered by the situation. Then read this interesting and inspiring story. Steven is a serious player in the Music Industry, has many years' experience and the ultimate respect of his colleagues. He has asked to remain anonymous so I'm not using his real name.

Going into the future exercise

'In 1994/95, I participated in a rigorous business leadership/executive education course consisting of four one week residential sessions over a period of nine months. This had a big impact in my performance at work.

'In the final week there was one exercise that was more free form than most of the other exercises. The idea was to go out into the future ten years hence, and as a free form stream of consciousness, write down where we were, who we were with, what it felt, tasted, smelled and looked like. These sensory notes were an important part of the exercise since they help lodge the idea not only in the mind, but in the body and emotions too.

'A clear picture came to me of a house on the beach with wooden pillars at the front that I thought was in the Caribbean. In the mental picture it was morning, my two children were coming to visit me at the house and I had a meeting with someone from the United Nations in the afternoon.

'Also during this exercise I visualised making enough money for my ex wife to have a decent sized house without a mortgage to provide more room for my two children and enough money for me to buy a place to live and not have the burden of a mortgage.

'In any case, I forgot about this whole exercise, and the notes that I had made, for many years.

'During the intervening period my second wife and I had

Marie Curie • Louis Pasteur • Hypatia • Oracle of Delphi

been introduced to a remarkable remote archipelago of islands on the East Coast of Kenya by our acupuncturist. We bought an acre of land on the beach and had a house built – a process that went surprisingly easily and had a magical feeling of "flow" in the whole process.

'Sometime after all this had happened I found my notes and realised that all three things in my "vision" had actually occurred in real life, and there were remarkable coincidences that the house was built just inside the ten year period since I'd done the exercise and also that the man who was at that time the husband of our acupuncturist actually worked for the United Nations.

'This whole experience had a very magical feeling about it, but at the same time had a sense of tapping into something very natural.'

I'd suggest that you might like to emulate the exercise that Steven was encouraged to do as part of his leadership training. It's a little-known fact that if you write something down it's 25% more likely to happen, and so it's possible that this 'forward projection' exercise has a powerful magic all of its own. Set a timescale for yourself; five or ten years hence are good benchmarks. Remember, let yourself be taken to a place that you'd never imagined; don't let current problems (such as financial issues, which are a bugbear even for the superrich) get in the way of your dreams and aspirations. Enter again that child-like state of mind where anything is possible, see what happens, write down the results, put into a sealed envelope then forget all about it and get on with the rest of your life.

Now let's look at some of the traditional ways of embarking on a spiritual quest. We can trigger some of these methods ourselves, whereas others seem to be down to the intervention of destiny.

Sir Christopher Wren • *Laurence Olivier* • *Bronwyn Bunt* • *Dante*

34

Fasting

What does it do to the body?
What does it do to the mind?
Why is it used for contacting angels
and other magickal work?

Fasting is the deliberate avoidance of food for a specified period, and has its roots in many different spiritual practices as well as being used as a means of detoxifying the body as a health treatment. However, a fast doesn't have to be restricted to food. Anything that we decide to abstain from is a fast; sexual activity, for example, or alcohol. Indeed, there are some Buddhists who further underline the rejection of the material world in that they refuse to handle money for certain periods of time.

Perhaps the most extreme form of fasting is the practice in the Jain faith known as Santhana. This is the very deliberate form of fasting in which the adherent effectively starves him or herself to death. Undertaken only when the individual feels that his purpose in life has been accomplished, this slow form of death gives the person plenty of time to reflect and prepare for the next world.

There's evidence that fasting is a practice that has been carried out for thousands of years; for example, The Prophet Mohammed is said to have fasted prior to the establishment of

Lynne Lauren • *Chrissie G* • *Adam Fuest* • *Jack White*

the Islamic faith, and of course devout Muslims fast during the month of Ramadan from dawn until dusk. The avoidance of food, drink and sex is a sign of respect for, and devotion to, God. There's evidence of fasting in other religious tracts, too; for example, the 40 days that Christ fasted in the desert, replicated in the 40 days of abstinence that follows the period of Lent in the Christian tradition, which is again similar to the 40 days' fast that was observed by Moses. Followers of the Vinaya school of Buddhism fast everyday from lunchtime to the following morning, as an aid to meditation, and Hindus fast often to show their devotion to a particular deity. There's solidarity in communal fasting that makes it easier; everyone is enduring the same difficulty, the same pain and the same hunger.

People fast as an atonement for perceived sins, to mourn and to show solidarity with the dead, and as a sign of gratitude to God.

Effectively, the removal of matter in the form of food is meant to take us away from the material world and directs us towards the spiritual. Even if you've missed a few hours without food you'll recognise the slightly heady, spaced feeling that results.

For the deliberate faster, the mental and emotional discipline involved in abstaining from food provides a great focus for the mind. Some fasters do so in order that wishes might be granted by showing the spirit world their intention; this idea is also followed sometimes by people who have fasted for political reasons, and a means of leverage; outing the self at risk of starvation in the aid of a cause can be a powerful and emotive weapon. Gandhi is a good example of this.

But what effect does fasting actually have on the body and the mind, and what has this got to do with angels?

Proponents say that fasting sharpens and focuses the mind, gives people clarity not gained when we eat 'normally', and can promote a general feeling of well-being and a lifting of the spirits. Cutting meat from the diet, too, can have the same effect, and further, so can excluding dairy and all other animal products. It's true to say that in general our diets in the West tend to be overloaded with chemicals and other toxins which our ancestors would never have experienced, so a chance to eliminate some of these substances from the system can only be a good thing. Conversely, fasting for too long a period, or without correct medical supervision, can make you tired and drowsy, susceptible to germs, light headed, forgetful and eventually quite ill. This isn't a medical tome so if you really want to try fasting as a way to communicate with angelic energies, please take proper supervision.

Here's a story from Elsa, a yoga practitioner from Germany.

'I hadn't actually been doing yoga for very long, but this was about 10 years ago and I got the bug as soon as I started. It was hatha yoga, and although I've tried many different kinds since then, for me hatha yoga is the essence, the best kind for me at least.

'The funny thing is that you start to think very differently about things once the connection between the body, the mind and the spirit are made. With me, perhaps the most important thing was that I could give up smoking without even thinking about it. I was already vegetarian, but found without even thinking about it that I had become virtually vegan after about 3 months of doing yoga every single day. Don't get me wrong, I'm not proselytising, everyone's experience is different – this is just what happened to me and as a yoga teacher now I can't afford to be too zealous since it can be off-putting.

'I decided to do a 10 day fast at the beginning of spring, the traditional time for a clear out, a spring-clean of the body if you like. I always think it's no accident that we have the religious observance of Lent at this time.

Mark Townsend • *Florence Nightingale* • *Roald Dahl* • *Ernst Haas*

'I should say at this point that I had proper supervision for the fast from my yoga teacher, who is still my teacher, and who is also a medical doctor. For the first three days I had to eat quite a lot of grapes and just water, which is tough, because by the third day the grape skins actually start to hurt your throat. Then it's just water for three days, then juice.

'I felt terrible by the fourth day; nauseous, achy, runny nose, and miserable. I found it hard sleeping because I was so hungry; I was dreaming about food. The fifth day wasn't great but on the morning of the sixth day I was feeling really good, like I'd been wrung out from the insides out, but really clear-headed and the hunger had thankfully abated.

'It was almost like I had to get through the pain of the previous days to attain this lovely feeling, a bit like climbing a steep mountain and then getting the fabulous view.

'I didn't meditate for the first five days – it would have been very difficult. My teacher asked me how I was feeling on the sixth day and when I told him I was feeling great, he instructed me to try meditating three times a day for the duration of the fast.

'On the ninth day I was doing my midday meditation and I had an immense feeling of calmness, beauty, an absorption into the universe, a true knowledge that everything was connected, and I was at the centre of this connection. I was concentrating all my focus into the third eye, and saw a tiny spot of brightness coming towards me. It was a tiny face, but highly detailed and very familiar. Gradually, the face drew closer and although it was so small the features were very clear. It was the face of an angel, that's all I can describe it as. And then I started to hear music, like a massive, soft, undulating string section, absolutely beautiful. Although my eyes were still closed, the brightness all around me was increasing and I felt utterly enveloped in light, love, calmness, peace, beauty. I sat in the lotus position for

Ansel Adams • Simone Johnson • Alan Card • Mike H • Judika Illes

maybe a couple of hours, tears streaming down my face, until the whole 'vision' faded, leaving traces of the music inside of my head. Then I slept like a baby for twelve hours.

'I know that this profound experience was a connection with angelic energies and that I was a part of these energies, everything connected, mind, body, soul, cosmos. I have fasted since and continued to do yoga, but what happened has never been repeated and I don't need it to. I didn't go looking for it. I feel very blessed to have had this experience.

'If this is what dying is like, then there's no need for anyone to have any fear of it.

'Was the experience brought about by the fasting? I have no doubt it had an important part to play, but that was a component part, not the only factor.'

I also asked Elsa how her life had changed after the experience.

'It's enriched me massively. I haven't told lots of people about it because I don't want it to be disseminated in the telling. Also, I'm aware that experiences like this, if discussed in the wrong place at the wrong time, can be alienating for people.

'But for myself, I know that the experience of the angels was real, and I understand from experience what many of the symbols of yoga and the Hindu faith are aimed at; symbols such as the lotus flower, with the petals forming multi-dimensional, encompassing rays, suddenly made sense in a very practical sort of way rather than just being images. I'm not Hindu, by the way – I suspect that all the sacred symbols in all religions point towards the same vision that I had, only we human beings choose to represent the idea in different ways.

'For me, I know that there's more to the world than we can see with our human eyes or hear with our human ears. If we

All the contributors to this book • James Lebon • Joni Mitchell

could experience those things in quite so much clarity the whole time, there would be no way we could operate, normally, in the material world. We wouldn't want to wake up from that dream.'

It's interesting that Elsa says that the fasting was only one factor in the angelic vision that she had. The yoga, the meditation, the breathing and the fasting seem to have created the perfect environment for it.

It makes sense, then to look next at just what a powerful tool meditation is in allowing angelic energies to flow through us.

Rhona Heath • Bobby Osborne • The Penponties • Lewis Carroll

35

Meditation – and the 'P' Word

There are many different forms of meditation, and it's up to you to experiment and see what works for you. David Lynch, who has practised Transcendental Meditation for many years and is a vociferous campaigner for its being introduced into schools, seems to be able to pull effortlessly on the creative and angelic energies of the universe.

The 'P' word is 'prayer', a word I'm reluctant to use because it does carry connotations of a very specific kind of spirituality. But if you take the essence of what prayer actually is – a focussed thought process – then you'll see that it is very closely connected with meditation.

This following story is once again from Steven, the music executive who features earlier in this chapter. The incident shows just how powerful these invisible energies can be.

Meditation Wasp Experience

'My wife and I were staying at Roydon Hall, a beautiful large manor house that the Transcendental Meditation movement

Zoroaster • *John Dee* • *Nancy Palmer-Jones* • *Adam Fuest*

used to have in Kent, one hour by train from London. My wife and I used to go there for deep rest meditation weekends called 'rounding' courses. These consisted of a series of yoga and simple breathing exercises and meditation to slow down the metabolism, yielding deep rest and a profound experience of peace. The house was used continuously for meditation and yogic flying courses and had a very settled atmosphere.

'On one occasion, in the summer, I was meditating in our bedroom, the window was open and a wasp came in. The meditation was very deep and I was experiencing very few thoughts, just a perfect stillness. The wasp was flying around and I had the thought to move it outside with my mind, so I held that intention and projected energy in the direction of the wasp with the message to it to move outside. To my surprise the wasp actually did move outside. I decided to attempt to make an energetic net or barrier to prevent the wasp coming back in, from where I was still sitting meditating. The wasp hovered outside the window, I removed the energetic barrier and the wasp came in through the window. I repeated the exercise to move the wasp out of the window and out it went.

'On the one hand this was surprising and there was also a feeling of being connected to something very natural, some kind of natural network that had embraced me or that the peacefulness of the whole environment had connected to.'

Does this last sentence sound very similar to the experience of universal connection experienced by Elsa? It seems that there's a connection between different forms of disciplines, whether they be mental (such as meditation) or physical (fasting, yoga, tai chi and other martial arts, for example). The same disciplines involved in complex dance movements, or musical skills, which turn off the 'chattering' part of the brain and allow the

Jeanne McKenzie • Robert Atherton • Doreen Virtue • Jacqui Newcombe

subconscious mind to come to the fore, also allow for the free flow of angelic energies, and a higher form of communication than mere words can usually allow.

Let's take a further look at how both prayer and meditation can affect us beneficially. There has been extensive research into the power of prayer. This research seems to prove that prayer does, indeed, work, although not always in the way we might expect. For those of us who might be squeamish about such religious-sounding terminology, see how it feels to replace the word 'prayer' with 'positive thought'. Apply the principles of such positive thinking to your own life and see what a huge difference it might make. It can be easy to get into the habit of thinking negatively about all the sorts of things that can befall us in our lives, and sometimes we need to do a sort of check and balance on our own mental attitudes.

First, does prayer actually work? If so, then how? And how can it put us in touch with angelic energies?

Asking questions like this really is like opening a can of worms. There are conflicting reports. And to be honest, I'm usually suspicious of the word 'prayer' as I've explained, since it's a bit too 'God Squad' for me. Followers of Richard Dawkins would argue that prayer wouldn't have any use or effect whatsoever. On the other hand, faithful devotees of any religion would argue the opposite.

What is true, however, is that when we make a conscious decision to think positively we become not only mentally better but our physical state can be affected, too.

It's incredibly difficult, though, to measure or quantify exactly how this works. It's almost impossible to find empirical evidence of such matters since anything which could even be defined as 'evidence' tends to be largely anecdotal. And until relatively recently the idea of doing experiments in which the term

Diana Cooper • *The Prophet* • *Roald Dahl* • *Paulo Coelho*

'prayer' was used, was anathema. Recently doctors in the UK were forbidden to pray for their patients, and yet there does seem to be evidence that such an act can be beneficial. This attitude is changing, however. For example, in the USA there's a body called the National Institute for Healthcare Research, which is conducting experiments into the effects of concentrated positive thoughts – which as we've seen is also known as prayer – in healing.

A recent experiment carried out by the Institute is interesting but still provides no conclusive evidence about the power of prayer. Possibly the most pertinent fact about the whole experiment is that it even happened in the first place.

Here's what happened. A patient about to undergo a tricky heart procedure (his third) was chosen as the focus for the prayers, mediations and good intentions of a large group of priests, monks, nuns etc scattered in various locations around the world. This group were given the name of the patient. The actual procedure could have easily resulted in a stroke, heart attack or even death. However, the patient survived the procedure although he had no idea that he was on the receiving end of so much positive energy.

Prayer and Meditation

Harvard scientist Herbert Benson has spent thirty years studying the effects of prayer and meditation. He points out that every religion has its own interpretation of the same basic idea often involving a mechanical device as an aid to focus; the Catholic rosary, the Buddhist mala, the worry beads seen in Mediterranean countries.

From these studies, Benson has found that any form of prayer makes the mind relax, de-stresses the individual and therefore

Jesus Christ • Jeremy Clarkson • Patti Smith • Tim Smit

promotes self-healing. The repetition of the words of a mantra is soothing and calming – and also focuses the mind on the intention carried by the sacred sounds whether or not the actual meaning is understood. MRI scans further show how the brain reacts during periods of intense meditation.

One of the effects is that the frontal and temporal lobes – those parts of the brain that govern self-awareness, distinctions between the self and the world, and which track time – become disengaged. At the same time, the limbic system becomes activated. This regulates relaxation, the autonomic nervous system, metabolism and blood pressure. Basically the relaxed state induced by meditation allows the system to do its job. The subsequent feeling of well-being and connection, awe and tranquillity that comes as part and parcel of the exercise may or may not come from a 'higher power'; if we're religious, we can attribute it to a god. If not, we can explain it as the mechanism of the mind.

Catherine's Story

Catherine Connors is a holistic therapist and meditation teacher, based between France and Ireland.

As with many people working in this sort of area, Catherine was 'drawn' to the work through a life-changing event. Before this event Catherine worked in the business sector and had a hectic lifestyle in which working a 17-hour day wasn't that unusual.

Then, 13 years ago, her mother became ill with cancer. Catherine returned to the family home in Ireland and was of course keen to do something practical to make her mother feel better. Her GP advised a course in massage; lymph drainage is an important factor in health, and so Catherine learned massage

Anita Roddick • *Alexandra David-Neal* • *Dalai Lama*

techniques so that she could apply them to her parent. The massage course triggered other areas of interest for Catherine and although her mother died four years later, Catherine's life took an about-turn as she turned away from the stresses of a life in business and towards holistic therapies.

'After my mother died, I never ever "felt" her. But my aunt and sisters said that they did. I was never upset that I didn't share this experience; I had always been the one that they called 'fiercely independent' in the family, never clingy, always making my own way. Possibly even stubborn! I never needed my mother for anything so I guess that this wouldn't need to change after she died, despite any experiences that other people might have had!

'Then, one day I had flown from Ireland to Paris, and was about to cross a very busy main road. Forgetting that the traffic was going to approach from the opposite direction to the one I was used to, I looked; saw nothing, stepped out into the road. Then to my surprise, I felt myself sharply tugged and lifted from behind. A huge bus zoomed past and unless the unknown person hadn't acted so swiftly and decisively I'd have probably been seriously injured, if not dead. I turned to say thanks – and there was no-one there. It all happened so quickly that I'd have seen if there was anyone in the vicinity; but there was seriously no-one there whatsoever.

'So, I finished what I had to do, went home, had a shower, and started to think about this strange event, trying to rationalise it in my head, trying to think of some sort of logical explanation for what had happened. As I was pondering, I "felt" my mother; there was no doubt about this presence, and unless you've ever truly had that sort of experience I'm aware of how strange this might sound. It felt that in all my fierce independence, she

Barack Obama • *Jules Verne* • *Frances Drake* • *Dylan Thomas*

showed up the one time she was needed and did something very practical to save my life.'

Strange and powerful though it is, Catherine's experience of being lifted away from danger is not unique. But is it possible that the ones that are do the lifting and pushing, actually angels? And if Catherine's belief that this unseen rescuer was indeed her mother, then would this make her mother an angel? These questions are impossible to answer.

Catherine went on to describe how, within the meditation groups that she teaches, there is a palpable energy that grows in the room. Some students have claimed to actually see these energies. In one particularly notable incident, a student who had arrived back at home was dazzled by bright lights through which she could discern the shape of wings. The experience was so profound that this particular person believed that she might have died, and has spent some time in trying to recapture the essence of that incredibly special moment.

'Meditation is a great means of becoming aware', says Catherine. 'Many people turn to meditation as a means of stress-control and relaxation. Whilst many are happy to stay at this level, for others, an awareness of their own sixth sense can start to happen.'

This realisation leads to belief, trust, and expansion into the 'otherworld', the realm of the imagination, the place of angels and infinite possibilities.

Lynne's Story

Lynne is an internationally-renowned psychic based in Cardiff, UK, and author of *Simply Meditation*. She also leads development circles and has the longest experience of meditation that I have

Robbie Burns   •   *T.S. Eliot*   •   *Jeremy Sandford*   •   *Bruce Chatwin*

ever come across outside the East or people from certain very particular religious or spiritual traditions.

'When I was growing up, my father was a great influence. Although he was an incredibly outspoken and vehement atheist, he taught me to meditate from the age of four, and this is a practice I continue to this day.

'Doing the sort of work I do, I see lots of interesting things that perhaps other people can't see. When something meaningful is going to happen, I've noticed there's a little sign. Someone may be sitting directly opposite me, and will then come and sit beside me. Whenever this happens, I think, aha, and wait to see what's going to transpire.

'One day I was leading a development circle, and I just went above everyone to check what was happening. I felt a presence beside me, and when I looked, the only way I can describe it is as a long, long tentacle of water; blue-white, moving light. I looked up and it went as far as I could see. I asked in my mind, 'Who *are* you?' and I heard the word, 'Michael'. This entity stayed for some time and seemed to be lending its energy to the group. I believe that we don't always see angelic beings in the classical wings and halo form!

'Another time, I was giving readings in Ireland when I was taken aback by an actual real, archetypal angel figure standing right in the middle of the circle. This was an amazing sight; a tall, beautiful figure, with floating wings, shining, shining bright light. I passed on some messages that were given to me by this figure, and when the lady asked where they had come from I was a bit reticent about saying, well, they are from a very tall, beautiful, bright white angel that is standing right here! Despite the awesomeness of these experiences, maybe it's good that we don't alarm people with them or make people believe we're utterly mad!'

Beryl Nozedar • *Trevor Nozedar* • *Andrew Catlin* • *Edith Piaf*

36

Imagination and Dreaming

The power of human imagination can never be under-estimated. Without it, the world would be a very different place. Essentially, everything we have invented started out as that small spark of imagination, from the wheel to a Hollywood blockbuster. Children are unafraid to explore their imaginary worlds, and adults, too, can gain a great deal by letting it soar.

Imaginary Friends?

'The parents always insisted on telling their child that their secret friends didn't exist — perhaps because they had forgotten that they too had spoken to their angel at one time. Or, who knows, perhaps they thought they lived in a world where there was no longer any place for angels. Disenchanted, the angels had returned to God's side, knowing that they could no longer impose their presence.'
—PAULO COELHO, *The Valkyries*

Did you have an imaginary friend, or friends, as a child? Do you have children who have this sort of a companion? If so, how about regarding this interesting phenomenon in a new light;

Billie Holiday • James Watt • Louis Armstrong • The Searys

that your child may be interacting with angelic energies, presenting in a strange, wonderful and non-threatening way? Children have the power of being more open to the invisible realms than adults, and who's to say that these companions, invisible to adults and often a source of both amusement and annoyance, are not angelic beings? These characters are not 'ordinary' and they are more common than we might realise; a recent survey from the USA found that 65% of children under the age of seven had such an ally. I know children that have numbered a blue cat, a talking dragon, a fairy, and a flying donkey amongst their imaginary friends. As bizarre though it might seem, there's an intensity about these sorts of relationships which can't be overlooked.

Exploring the Invisible Realms

Angels don't always appear to us in the bright light of day; they can reveal themselves in dreams, thoughts, meditations. We've already discussed how angelic energies interact with human energies to inspire creative thought. The following story Chrissie's, an artist specialising in textiles. The visions that she brings into her life have many archetypal images and symbols in them.

Chrissie's Story

'When I'm preparing for a piece of artwork, I go off on what I call my "travels". The first place I come to is a garden. The garden isn't exactly on the "other side"; it's more of a transitional, intermediary place. In the garden are people that have "passed over;" i.e. those that we think of as dead. There are no people there that I know to be "alive".

Theo   Chalmers   •   Janet   Gleghorn   •   Edmund   Hilary

'There's a pool with an apple tree. I go down into the pool, underwater, and into a cavern. In the cavern is more water. This, then, is the "underworld".

'I go over the stream and into a cave where I know that something profound is going to happen. It is here that I find the figure that I call 'Michael'. Michael is very, very bright, too bright to look at directly. This light, I know, is often interpreted as wings, but to me it is as though he is actually constructed of light. I can't look. The brightness is, literally, "awesome".

'I am invited to lie on a sort of stone slab. Michael's hands are above my head, but not touching. As I lie there, all the rubbish and dirt and dis-ease are flushed out of my body and through my feet. I am somehow cleansed. All my grief is taken away and I feel whole again'.

Chrissie goes on to explain other parts of her meditation, things that occur unbidden.

'In another place, I meet a female entity who I know is an aspect of myself. A muse, if you like. She takes me into a meditation in which I am handed a golden apple and a silver pear. I take these fruits into a garden. There's a bowl, with water in it and I place the apple and the pear on either side of the bowl.

'The frequency rises. There's a misty film over the top of the bowl and when I look into the water I can see symbols, shapes without words attached. I wait, and then something appears in the bowl which I can lift out. The thing is a symbol, a sort of key.

'Then I am taken to a cliff face with many niches, each with a door. The symbol matches that on one of the doors. Inside, the little alcove has an object in it which is available to me. This is not an exact representation of the object – it's the essence of an idea of the object'.

Douglas Bader • *Elvis* • *Grace Darling* • *Rosa Parks*

Chrissie goes on to describe how she brings the object back into the 'real world' with her, examines it again, and then makes the actual object; this is the inspiration for her art. But the process doesn't end there. Once made, Chrissie repeats the process from the beginning, at the Garden of the Dead, taking the object back to the little cavern where it came from. There, she symbolically places the finished object back where it came from, making the circle of creation complete and whole.

I was particularly struck with the Chrissie's story. In it, she goes through a process of spiritual purification brought about by an entity that she describes as 'Michael'. This entity has all the hallmarks of an angelic being – the name, the intensely bright light, the appearance of wings, the evident healing energies – but Chrissie does not describe him as such. She describes the appearance, but never makes any claims for exactly what this being is. It is interesting to note, however, that Chrissie's recent work does feature angelic forms quite prominently.

Angels of the Dreamtime

In which other ways do angels communicate with us? A very obvious answer is through dreams.

We know that, like any other spirits, angels are unlikely to appear to us in any guise which is likely to be alienating, frightening or alarming. Some of us might be prepared for a complete revelation, but most of us are not. Therefore angelic communications are frequently veiled, abstruse, elliptical, unexpected. This makes the dream the perfect vehicle. The tricky bit is actually remembering the details of the dream!

There's a historical precedent of human beings being given inspiration from the spiritual world during sleep. For example, Joseph Smith, founder of the Mormon faith, is generally

Christian Barnard · Simon Clayton · Esti Clayton · Linda and Dominic

accepted to have been given the information in The Book Of Mormon from divine sources, revealed in a dream, although it's unlikely that we'll ever know for sure whether Smith was, as is often rumoured, a ceremonial magician. If he was, this means that he may have been able to summon angelic entities.

Then there's the story of the great poet, Coleridge. Two or three hundred lines of his epic poem, *Kubla Khan*, came to him entirely in a dream. He was busy scribbling down the lines when he was famously interrupted by the arrival of an unexpected visitor, 'a person on business from Porlock'. Incidentally, Coleridge had taken some kind of drug to help him sleep since he was feeling ill; it wouldn't be a surprise if this had been some kind of opiate.

The weird thing about dreams is that, when we're dreaming, we're usually unaware of the fact. That is, except for the phenomenon called 'lucid dreaming', those rare examples in which we actually can tell the difference between the real world and the dream one and can start to take control of what's happening. Lucid dreams can be the most delightful kind, often involving us being able to fly or perform other superhuman feats. Additionally, dreams can often enable us to come up with solutions to problems that our waking minds cannot solve. The next time you have a puzzling issue or concern and someone tells you to 'sleep on it' they're saying this for a very good reason. Often, a solution that will not reveal itself during the hard cold light of day can appear, as it were, in the morning, on the pillow beside you. In fact, it's well worth trying. That master of the dream world, CG Jung, said that once our subconscious mind knew that we wanted to 'play', then it would make its communications more accessible to us and easier to access. That simple notepad and pencil beside the bed is as good a start as any because, like angels, the contents of dreams, too, can be elusive.

Marco Polo • Alex Maiolo • Stanley Meyer • Nikola Tesla

Unless we make a deliberate effort to record the contents of whatever we can remember immediately on waking, the details, information feeling and memory that comprised the dream can fizzle away like so many champagne bubbles.

Angels in Dreams

We go yet again to the Bible to find an early example of angelic aid coming via the mechanism of a dream. 'Jacob's Ladder' is the tale in which Jacob fled the wrath of Esau. He had to stop for the night in a place called Haran. That night Jacob had a vivid dream, a dream of a ladder with its foot on the Earth and its top far out of reach up in the clouds. Angels were travelling up and down this extraordinary ladder, and Jacob was able to accurately interpret the meaning of this dream. It seems that this ability ran in the family. Jacob's son, Joseph, became famous not only for remembering his own dreams, but interpreting those of others. Typically, his dreams were rich with symbols, which are a universal language running far deeper than any written or spoken language.

Joseph's dreams – and his interpretation of them – caused problems. In one such dream, he was working in the fields with his brothers when his own sheaf of corn rose up higher than the others. This didn't go down well, and when Joseph subsequently showed the sun, moon and stars bowing down to him, he was packed off, and sold as a slave before the arrogance that his father and brothers thought he was suffering from, overwhelmed him. However, even this subsequent humiliation as a slave, and his imprisonment after rejecting the advances of the wife of Potiphar, were unable to stop him from fulfilling his destiny; indeed, it was in prison that his skill in dream interpretation really started to blossom. His fame reached the

Lynne Lauren • *Tylluan Penry* • *Bill Gates* • *Warren Buffett*

ears of the Pharaoh and Joseph's destiny was sealed. It's interesting to observe here how Joseph had no choice but to 'go with the flow' and all his difficult circumstances conspired to put him in exactly the place he needed to be.

In the flurry of attention that's placed upon Mary, Joseph's difficult role is often overlooked. And yet he is reassured in a dream. In this dream, an angel appears to him, and tells him not to have any concerns about making Mary his wife despite her pregnancy, and the full situation, that his betrothed is bearing the child that was conceived by the Holy Ghost, is clarified for him. Joseph is also told that the ensuing child will be rather special. We are not given the specific name of this angel; it is described only as 'the angel of the Lord'. Further along in the story, it's an angel that appears again to Joseph and tells him to flee with Mary and Jesus to Israel to save the life of his child. It is not explained whether this angel appeared in a dream or not, but the warning was taken seriously. Elsewhere in the Bible, Pilate's wife is warned that her husband should try to stop the persecution of Jesus. She tells him; 'Have nothing to do with that just man; for I have suffered many things this day in a dream because of him' (Matthew 27:19).

Dreams of Angels

Angels are, as we have seen, laden with symbolism, a powerful archetype. Although the interpretation of dreams relies to a great extent on context, we can safely say that the angel as a symbol represents the heavenly realms, goodness, morality, protection, guardianship. We can't overlook their role as messengers from the Spirit, either. Some people believe that angels appear in dreams around the time of a birth or a death within the close circle of family and friends.

Prof Alan Jones • Phillip Carr-Gomm • Stephanie Carr-Gomm

Dreams that come directly from angels sometimes 'feel' different from other dreams. They have a clarity about them that often isn't an attribute of the usual dreams which may be nothing more than a sort of psychological filing system trying to make sense of the events of the day. Dream messages that come directly from the subconscious are dripping with strange symbolism; ones from angels will have the symbolism and also an uplifting feeling of tranquillity and 'anything is possible'. Your angel may not always appear as such, but the feeling will be consistent – once it happens for the first time you'll always recognise it. Birds are also symbolic of messengers from the spiritual realms, so keep a note of any birds that appear in your dreams. It's also likely that the angel might appear as a nature spirit; don't be afraid to keep an open mind.

Because angels also represent the higher aspects of our mind, the 'oneness' of the universe, angel dreams may be about your own self-realisation, or may herald a time of karmic balance that goes beyond the ego. And above all, bear in mind that angels can herald the changes that need to happen in our lives in order for us to make a transition; if we are in a rut of our own making and not 'on the path', an angel can be a reminder that something is going to happen to jolt us back onto the right route. This might not always be easy, but once the ball is rolling there's nothing you can do to stop it!

How to Welcome Angels Into Your Dreams

There's an awful lot to be said for that simple notepad and pencil beside the bed. It shows the subconscious mind that you're ready to meet it halfway, to 'play back'. But this might not happen overnight; remember, communication has to be a two-way thing.

Yuri Gagarin • *Buddy Holly* • *Ennio Morricone*

It's also important to prepare yourself and your surroundings psychologically for an angel dream. Presumably you're going to be doing your dreaming in your bedroom, so make sure that it is thoroughly cleaned, both physically and psychically. Smudge all corners, nooks and crannies of the room with a sweet-smelling incense or, better still, a sage stick. Take special care to make sure that any reflective surfaces such as mirrors and windows are sparkling clean.

You could bring in your angel altar to the room as a focus for your attentions. Make sure it's replenished with fresh flowers and again, burn some sweet-smelling incense.

Bathe before going to sleep. Then, as it's getting dark, light a candle on your altar (remember that it's likely you'll fall asleep before the candle burns out so make sure it's safe to carry on burning – a candle in a jar is fine so long as there's nothing hanging over it that might catch light).

Before you go to sleep, set you alarm clock for a time earlier than you would usually awake. Very often a sudden awakening is a good catalyst to remembering dreams.

Then, lie back, do some breathing exercises, concentrate on your candle and ask, out loud, for you angel to come to you. You might have a specific problem that you would like to ask about; make it succinct, don't waffle. Then simply relax, fall asleep, and write down everything that you remember when you are awoken. Bear in mind that dream messages are liable to come to us in symbols rather than in a very straightforward way. These symbols may not mean anything at first, but keep up the exercise and see what transpires over the days, weeks and months.

This is important stuff and can't be rushed. Yes, you might get lucky and make contact immediately – but that might not be your path. Keep trying, it's worth the effort.

David Lynch · Amy Johnson · Donald Campbell · Amelia Earhart

Having looked at some of the things we can do to deliberately encourage angelic energies, let's now look at some of the strange things that life throws at us — seemingly randomly — to trigger the higher part of our mind.

John Morris • *Ron Edwards* • *David Lynch* • *Henry Miller*

37

Past Lives?

Angels often appear to us when we're not looking for them and when we least expect them. This might be when we are under medical sedation or perhaps hypnosis, as is the case in the following incident.

There are different ways of looking at the business of past lives. One is where we look into our earliest years to find the reasons for our current mental states and traumas. Another is when we go beyond, into lives we have supposedly had before the current one. The possibility for such past lives opens up a hornets' nest of conflicting theories and possibilities, but despite the speculative nature of such experiences, there's no doubt that they can be very profound to the person experiencing them. I had hesitated to use such an anecdote in this book, but the source of this next one is 100% reliable and comes from a person of great integrity.

Lisa's Story

Lisa J is a highly-successful tour manager who works with some of the leading musical artists in the world, as well as working on

Doug and Joy • *Ellen Macarthur* • *Jont* • *Oppenheimer*

the Olympics and the MTV awards. She tends to spend most of her time living out of her Samsonite suitcase and there are very few parts of the world which haven't been graced with her presence over the years.

A cool, steady head and a calm demeanour are prerequisites for someone in Lisa's position. She needs to remain sober and in control at all times no matter how hard the party might be going on around her. Lisa is not in the least fanciful or 'ditsy', but embraces everything and isn't closed to any possibilities. Fundamental to this inner calm are yoga and meditation, and Lisa practises both wherever she is in the world.

Recently, though, her spiritual life took an interesting turn when she, quite spontaneously, encountered her own guardian angel.

'I'd gone for a Past Life Therapy session, purely in the interests of trying to find out why I seem to keep making the same mistakes in relationships', said Lisa. 'I knew that Past Life Regression and Past Life Regression Therapy were two different things, one a means of delving into the past as evidence of survival, the other a means of analysis that allows us to see past events in a different light and to help us get out of a rut in terms of life experience, mistakes, etc. It was definitely the latter process that I was interested in'.

We don't need to go into all of Lisa's experiences whilst she was put into a light hypnotic state; they are not only very personal, but also not really relevant here.

'The therapist at one point told me to take the incidents that had 'gone wrong' in the past and offer them up to my 'higher self' in order to mend them. She told me also to picture my higher self, and at the moment of the suggestion I was faced

Freud • Jung • You • Picasso • Lyn and Margaret Regan

with an angelic-type being; I distinctly remember that she was wearing a very well-cut A-line dress. She asked me what part of myself needed to be healed and I found myself answering, quite confusingly, "Pity". It's true that I have often got involved with people and situations because I feel pity for them. The angel grabbed my face, kissed me, and said, "Pity is not compassion".

'This small sentence has released a profound understanding in me. Pity means that we find ourselves getting caught up in other people's problems, often for all the wrong reasons. Whereas compassion means that we can extend our senses and "feel" for the person or the situation, we can empathise with it without needing to assert our ego.

'At the time, I must admit that I didn't want to leave my angel; I wanted to stay with her, but now I have grown to understand that she's with me all the time.'

Me • *Ptolemy* • *JK Rowling* • *JRR Tolkien*

38

Illness as a Catalyst

Ancient cultures believed that the Shaman of the tribe, the person with the mystical connection to the other world, who could commune with spirits, heal the sick and divine the future, needed to go through a sort of baptism of fire in order to sharpen and refine these powers. In this particular story, illness acted as similar catalyst, triggering powers and talents that Jane MacDonald had never known about. Jane is a reiki healer and lives in the USA.

Jane's Story

'Up until five years ago I had a very conventional life. I lived in a nice semi and had a good job in the civil service. My husband was a chef (in fact he still is!) and my two daughters were doing well at the local school.

'Then I was diagnosed with cervical cancer. Just the thought of the C word was the most frightening thing that had happened to me. The rug really was pulled from under my feet.

'My husband and girls were fabulous, but the deeper I got into

Pablo Casals • Jaqueline DuPrey • Maria Callas • Carl Sagan

the treatment the more I started to have the feeling that something major was missing from my life which, on the surface, would appear to be perfect. But I didn't know what this thing was.

'One day during a course of treatment, and feeling at the lowest ebb ever, I was sitting alone in my ward, and one of the cleaning orderlies came in. It was obvious that I'd been crying. The cleaner came up and offered me a glass of water and a tissue, which I took. Then she asked what was wrong, and the whole thing came pouring out of me; I had everything and loved my family, but something was missing and I had cancer – *I had cancer* – so what could I do about it? Then this person sat down on the edge of the bed, put her arm around my shoulder and started to stroke my forehead.

'She said, "It's time to be who you really are. This illness will go away and you will see that there was a reason for it. It's never about the actual illness. Go to sleep and maybe you'll dream of the missing thing".

'And then I did actually fall into quite a deep sleep, and weirdly, I did dream of the missing thing. In my dream, I saw this same cleaner except that she was very bright; an angel. I was suddenly filled with hope, a sense of possibilities, and an idea that there was something within reach.

'I knew that some major transformation had taken place. It was no problem for me to cut anything out of my life that was less than satisfying or which wasn't contributing to the bigger picture, and as I started to recover I quit my job whilst I still had this resolve.

'I did recover from the cancer, and realised that I had healing powers of my own. I studied everything, but find that reiki is the most effective and that the energies I use in my healing are directly connected to the angelic realms that I was introduced to that day. There's no mistaking that feeling.

Jonathan Cainer • Dame Margot Fonteyn • Nureyev • The Heathies Ghandi

'I wouldn't say that I am a different person, but I am a more honest person. I never saw that cleaner again during all my time in the hospital and whilst it might be fanciful to suggest that she was a real angel, to be honest nothing would surprise me any more.

'If it hadn't been for the cancer, I doubt that I would have had the courage to change things so dramatically. When we stand on the precipice, we have to jump, and it's then that we realise we can fly.'

Greg's story

Greg Suart is a UK-based personal coach and inspirational speaker. He's yet another example of a high-achiever that is not afraid to talk about angels, and is open about his experiences with them. Greg's 'awakening' also took place after a serious illness, and put him in direct contact with angelic energies.

'When I was a kid, I used to go to Mass every day. Although the trappings and all the pomp didn't make sense to me, I was always aware that there was "something else" going on, aside from all the narrow mindedness and bigotry. But my experience of the power of angels and angelic energies came about as a result of several "trigger" events, if you will.

'For nearly two years, I had chronic repetitive injury stress in both arms. During that time I went through phases where I couldn't drive, hold a book or even wash my own hair. The pain I had was constant whenever I was active – and so, I was forced to be still. I went to see a "normal" GP who wanted to put both my arms in plaster casts! I knew that this wasn't the solution since it was important that I did continue to use the muscles; apart from this, it would have rendered an already difficult life nigh-on impossible.

• *Stephen Hawking* • *Mother Teresa* • *Peter Sellers*

For 18 months I tried just about every single alternative therapy going. Reiki, acupuncture, acupressure, massage, psychic surgery, healing; you name it, I tried it. Some of the therapies seemed to work for a while, but nothing was really sorting me out or getting to the real core of the problem. But I promised myself that I *would* find a cure.

I view this illness as a catalyst for everything that's happened since, and in many ways I'm actually grateful for it.

'Then someone gave me two books; *You Can Heal Your Life* by Louise Hay, and also *Light Up Your Life* by Diana Cooper. In a state of despair, and barely able to hold a book open, I immersed myself in both titles and concluded that if there was *anything* in what they contained then I would at least tee off in a golf competition in three weeks time. The work included a lot of meditation and visualisation and, most importantly, being honest with myself. As Veronica (my healer, who gave me the books) said to me: "Your ego wants to do one thing and your soul another, your body is the battle ground – sort it out!" I realised that I had to change the inner self in order to cure the outer. As it turned out I played two days of golf without repercussions – I had begun to get how I create the reality that I call my life and how I can also heal it.'

Do you know how long it was before Greg had that round of golf? Three weeks. Just three weeks, after years of being crippled with pain. Not only that, but he enjoyed two whole days of golf and hasn't suffered pain since. Greg then went on to discover angels.

'I'd always been seeking and questioning, and like to think that I have an open mind. Because of the books I'd read, I decided that I'd simply call on angels to come and help me. It was as

Tony Benn • *Joanna Lumley* • *Keir Hardie* • *T E Lawrence*

simple as that. Now, I regularly call on Raphael and Michael for specific reasons. They're there; they exist, they're a part of my life. It doesn't matter whether you call them angels, angelic energy, ascended masters or divine forces. These divine forces are moving toward our consciousness, and work with us on all levels – physical, emotional, mental, spiritual.

'There's another book that I'd recommend highly, *The Tibetan Book of Living and Dying*. Bizarrely, this book actually helped me make sense of Christ's teachings – which is kind of curious given that the Buddhists record him to be a Yogi Master of the highest order who spent a number of years in the East between the ages of 12 and 30 – a period not recorded in the Bible!'

Richard Burton • Finlay, Janette and Tyler • George Harrison

39

Allowing For Possibilities and Asking Questions

I t struck me that many of the contributors to this book, the people who have had encounters with angelic energies, are involved in the creative arts, or otherwise have a lateral approach to life. Perhaps it's this receptivity which helps in recognising the invisible world. We all have talents in different areas, and an open mind – whilst retaining a level of sensibility – means that we can evaluate possibilities in a fairer way than someone with absolutely fixed and set ideas.

Retaining a child-like state of mind

You know how children will soak up new ideas like a sponge? Imagine if we can retain that same sense of wonder and possibility whilst retaining our adult knowledge of what is and is not true.

The fact is that we cannot disprove nor prove the existence of

Terry Gilliam • *David Lean* • *Michelangelo* • *Jim Morrison*

a God; it is also difficult to prove or disprove the possible existence of angels. It seems, therefore, reasonable to allow for the possibility of either and both, but to be aware that they might not present themselves to us in any way that we might have come to expect from what we've read about or seen in the movies. Things aren't black and white. Here's a very simplistic analogy.

Adults tell their children that there's a character called Santa Claus, who brings gifts at Christmas time. The children believe in this figure, around which there's a very beautiful and imaginative set of stories. Gradually, it comes to light that it is in fact the parents who play the role of Father Christmas, and it's they who leave the presents beneath the tree or under the bed or wherever. For the child, up until the time when they learn the truth, the result is the same; they believe in a possibility, and they get presents. Once the children are old enough to learn the truth, that the parents had taken on the role of this generous character, it's almost as though they undertake a sort of initiation; it's lovely to see how older siblings will keep alive this story as long as they can with their younger brothers and sisters.

Does this mean that Santa Claus doesn't exist? No – far from it! Santa is conceptually a work of genius and is no more or less real than God.

What if, here in the material world, we work with a bunch of myths, stories and imaginative possibilities that serve their purpose until such a time as we are ready to move on to the next phase of existence?

Here's a story from Catherine, a former nun who lives and works in Scotland.

'When I was a child I believed incredibly strongly in Santa Claus. I used to lie in bed, thinking I was awake all night but

Frank Capra • Yoav • Kelly Joe Phelps • Otis Redding

can't have been, sweating with nerves in case I either saw him by accident or he didn't come at all. One year I actually heard sleigh bells on the roof and footsteps on the stairs; I was so terrified that I put my head under the covers and trembled with fear and excitement. I swear that the sounds I heard were real!

'This might sound really weird, but my calling to become a nun was mixed up with this childhood possibility, i.e. the possibility that Santa exists, and my decision to leave the Order was also a part of the same thing.

'I realised that the actual belief in the existence of Santa was what mattered. It encourages children to take notice of right from wrong, to aspire to correct behaviour, to be the best they can be in return for material gain – something that is understandable to, and accessible to, a child.

'In the same way, there's an idea of a heaven and hell that might well do the same thing; encourage us to be the best that we can be in order to go to a good place after we die rather than a bad place. This started to sit uncomfortably with me; it became more of a political doctrine than an actual reality, metaphysical or otherwise. Does the belief in Santa make for a better world? Yes. Does the belief in a God do the same thing? Yes, I think so. But where other human beings use this quite natural belief in an overriding intelligence and meaning to everything as a means of gaining power and control over others – as can be the case, unfortunately, with the Church – then I don't think that this is right. I still believe in my own version of this intelligence, and a part of me still believes in Santa – but my ideas went a long way away from the required mode of thinking and I felt uncomfortable. So I left.'

The Buddha • *Otis Redding* • *Neil Young* • *Jeff Beck*

40

Taking Risks

OK, we've already seen how the free flow of truth and ways of reminding ourselves that we are connected with the universe are synonymous with working with angelic energies.

These techniques are all very well as theories, but it's not always easy to follow them; we go in ups and downs, different levels of awareness.

Have you ever noticed that when you climb out of your comfort zone – whether by accident or design – things often go better than you might have expected? The occasions I'm talking about are the ones that usually fill us with dread. You might have lost a job or been made redundant. Perhaps you've been offered a promotion. It could be something very significant and life-changing or something small, such as having to face a room full of strangers at a party. All these things can either happen to us *or* we can somehow cause them to happen with a level of awareness. It doesn't matter. After all, we have to face these things all through our lives, from the first day at school onwards. In the same way that this first day in a strange environment leads to our learning and making progress as human beings, so it is that

Carlos Castenada · *David Attenborough* · *Brian Eno* · *Peter Gabriel*

our risks, our mistakes, our different ways of daring to try something new all do the same thing.

These times, which can seem like we are about to freefall through our own lives, seem to offer ample opportunity for our angelic energies, helpers, call them what you like – to kick in. Where the synchronicities come in is when we need a reminder that we are actually doing the right thing.

Some people are natural-born risk takers, love that feeling of being metaphorically on the edge of the cliff, ready to jump off and either fall to the ground or fly up to the sky. But for others it's difficult. It's a fact that most multi- millionaires will have made some terrible mistakes and may even have been made bankrupt one, if not more, times. Sometimes, what we take for failure actually can provide an invaluable life-lesson that can lead to success – whatever we choose to see it as.

Sometimes, the jolt that we are given by the universe can seem to be a very cruel one. But we have it in our power to turn the most horrendous of events into a gift. The following story is the epitome of this idea.

Rhiannon and Ella's Story

'Ella's gift to me was to make my world much bigger so I could see life in a different way. She taught me to trust and helped me to understand that life isn't always easy, but it's good. Through her I realised that nothing is separate; everything is connected in love, and everything is possible. We are here to learn to live in love, to discover our potential as human beings, to use our gifts – and to enjoy the journey!'

Rhiannon is a health practitioner who lives in a very beautiful, remote and rural part of Wales. Her personal philosophy of life

Bob   Geldof   •   Bono   •   John   Martyn   •   Chrissie   Hynde

– which is amongst the most uplifting, encouraging and soul-seeking of any I have ever come across – was forged as a result of one of the most heartbreaking and traumatic of experiences; the death of her baby, Ella. Rhiannon's courage is an utter inspiration and reminder of the power of the human spirit. This story is also full of angels and angelic energies, and for Rhiannon, the ultimate realisation that it is possible to make something very, very good out of something that seems to be very, very bad indeed.

'I'd had what I suppose would be called a very comfortable and conventional upbringing; a secure, loving family, enough for all our needs financially. I think I'd had it very easy; anything I wanted, I could reach out and get for myself, pretty much. In retrospect, there were no challenges within my family at that time that required any sort of faith. This is something I've learned over time.

'Then, when I was 40, everything changed. I was due to be married and my partner left me with no real explanation. Soon after, I realised I was pregnant and I carried my daughter for nine months with love and hope; she was my future. Then, just before she was born, Ella died.

'They could give me no reason, no medical cause, she had just bled in to me and gone to sleep. The midwives who delivered Ella and saw me through those first few days were wonderful, so was the consultant, who offered me these words: "There are some things that we can never understand, but which we just have to accept..."

'But it made no sense to me. All our lives we are brought up to believe that if we are good, then good things happen. I had been good, or as good as I knew how to be, all my life. Why, then, had this terrible thing happened? I was utterly broken.

'What kept me going was a small voice inside of me, telling

Brancusi • George Best • Pele • Django Reinhardt • Sherpa Tensing

me, "You have to stay open". And somehow, despite my huge grief, I knew I had to honour that voice.

'Instinctively part of me understood that the *only* way that I could get through was to give in; and I said to the small voice, take me wherever you will.

'From that point on, I found that I had all the support that I needed. I was given so much love, from family, friends, total strangers offering words of comfort. I remember my window cleaner; all he did was touch my hand, but it was as though he touched my soul through his compassion and understanding.

'And all the time I was questioning my existence, asking, "Who am I? What am I? and what am I doing here?"

'I threw everything in the air. I gave up my job and sold my house. I went wherever I felt was right. I listened to that voice. Somehow, deep down, I knew that I had to remain open, in order to keep the connection of the profoundly deep and pure love that I had forged with my daughter. I had to surrender to it.

'I was put in touch with an amazing bereavement counsellor, who enabled me to explore my feelings and thoughts. I got the sense that she was giving me just enough of what I needed to find things out for myself.

'The first place I visited on my journey was Findhorn in Scotland, from there I went on to the island of Erraid, and then onto the island of Iona. It was funny; the moment I set foot on Iona I knew that I had 'come home' and that the island was exactly where I needed to be at that time. My grief was still all-consuming, but I retained an open heart. Having arrived at Iona, I wanted to stay in the Abbey, but there was no room. In the queue there was a woman in front of me who was also trying to make sense of recent events in her life, and she had asked specifically to have a room to herself, which was the last room available. The administrators had a word with her about me and

Alexandra David-Neal • *Miles Davis* • *David Tomlinson*

she did the most amazingly generous thing; she offered to share her room with me, a total stranger.

'Later I became a volunteer on the island, and stayed there for a number of months, continuing my healing. It was an extraordinary and generous experience.

'Gradually, I realised and accepted that Ella was my gift; not the one that I had thought she would be, but nevertheless, a gift.

'When I came back to Wales, about a year after Ella's death, I rented a place in a very beautiful part of the Brecon Beacons. A few miles down the road was a completely derelict house which I passed fairly frequently. It was literally tumble down; three walls, nearly, and no roof to speak of.

'One Monday I passed by and there was a sign by it saying that it was for sale by auction that same Friday, just five days later. I thought at the time that it must be a "fix". The owner of the cottage I was staying in was a wonderful man called Richard, and he kept saying to me, "Go look!" I did, and the old farmhouse was even worse than I'd realised. Added to the equation was the fact that it had no water or electricity.

'As I walked to the gate there was a robin; I always associated this little bird with Ella, and took it as a sign from her. As I walked back, there was a whole family of robins. This was a definite sign that I was on the right track.

'So, I went to the auction. Very few people knew that I was going to go, and I had certainly not told my immediate family. I'd had some advice about only bidding at the end, and knowing exactly how much you could spend. All the time on the way to the auction, I was asking; give me a sign, a sign, a sign!

'The auction was held in a very modern hotel in Cardiff Bay. The house was the last lot. The auction was held in the ballroom, and as I looked around it I realised that there were angels painted all around the walls. This felt like the sign I'd been asking for.

David McAlmont • *Glenn Miller* • *Danny Kaye* • *Chi Fi Masters*

'I didn't bid straight away, but right at the end as I'd been advised. Although I'm small and I know that people see me as feminine, the auctioneer referred to me as "the man at the back". Then when I had to bid again, they had obviously decided that I was definitely female, and I'll never forget the auctioneer's words as he said, "Sold to the lady wearing a poppy!"

'A man came up to me and said how glad he was that I'd bought the house, and told me that my face had lit up when it happened. I had to pay a deposit, and my hand was shaking so much that I could hardly write the cheque.

'My parents were in Cardiff, so I decided I'd better go straight over and tell them what I had done. Only my father was in, and he was surprised to see me since I hadn't told them I'd be coming over. I took a deep breath and told my father that I'd just bought a completely derelict house in a remote part of the Brecon Beacons.

'My father, a very conservative, "proper" man, said something that I really hadn't expected. He said, "Oh, darling, I'm so pleased for you. This is your new beginning". On the other hand, my mother's reaction, of sheer horror and huge concern for my sanity, wasn't a surprise at all! Though, to be fair, she soon came around too. My father loved the space, and helped plant trees and thought a lot about the garden. He was great.

'I keep on seeking and searching, but the more I do so, the more I realise that there are no answers. I have become more accepting of everything and anything that happens. Life goes on, and has its challenges. We have to make our life journey in faith – faith in the universe – so that whatever happens, whatever is put in front of us, we accept that it is sent as a gift to teach us whatever it is that we need to learn. However difficult that might seem.

'Once we are "woken up", it's impossible to deny it, or go

Gustave Klimt • Gustave Holst • Vaughan Williams • Stravinsky back. It won't let you, otherwise everything becomes meaningless. It's part of really learning to live, and that we are really "in" it, every moment that we have. All I did was to make a conscious effort to open myself, and everything else happened effortlessly. Life did everything for me. We have to surrender, and accept.

'I am hugely grateful to have my daughter. Ella didn't even take a breath; she is a pure spirit. I have had to look hard in the mirror, take a raw look at what I've become and all the ways I've justified certain things. In that way our connection has grown stronger and stronger. She has taught me the meaning of love and we journey together as spiritual beings; me with my feet firmly planted on the ground, grounding the energy we share!

'I was given a good piece of advice. Initially, when we are awoken, it's as though we are a spindly little sapling. We need to learn how to protect ourselves. Then as we grow and get stronger, we can test our courage.

'And we need to stay "light". Life is meant to be enjoyed. It's easy to get too "heavy".

'Angels are made of light, and they fly. Being in the moment is the only way to connect with the angels outside ourselves, as well as the ones inside.'

Rhiannon's story has ended happily. The family of robins that she took as a sign that cold November day outside the derelict house, proved to be a prophecy. Today, after huge amounts of energy, determination and love, the house is a beautiful home for Rhiannon, her husband, and her little boy. She continues her journey, ever open to where it will take her next.

Beethoven • *Heinrich Biber* • *Rudolf Steiner* • *Paganini*

41

Being Courageous
and Facing the Truth

Have you ever had the feeling that your life is in a rut, yet you are unsure about how to get out of it? Perhaps you're bored in a well-paying but tedious job. Maybe you're living in a place which simply doesn't make you happy but which is convenient for the aforementioned job. We might be in an unhappy marriage, but rather than face the truth and speak to one another we have affairs in an attempt to escape.

Why do people stay in these situations? If this is you, what are *you* staying in this situation for? Unhappiness and depression can often be indicators that we're not living in the truth, not paying heed to our own feelings. This can lead to physical and mental illnesses and can create a circular pattern of frustration and anger.

Question everything!

The reason we stick with these life-deadening situations is generally down to fear: fear of making a change, fear of the unknown, fear of disruption and insecurity. And yet, what's the worst thing that can happen? Once you've had some kind of baptism of fire, once you've been through something truly

Carlos Santana · W B Yeats · William Blake · Ted Hughes

terrible — loss of a loved one, a serious illness — it seems somehow easier to take risks, to throw things up in the air and see where they land.

One of the other weird things that people do is to hoard money. I'm not talking about the necessity to put money aside for general living expenses, but about the people that hang onto money rather than using it to buy freedom and experiences. Again, this comes from a place of fear. Wouldn't it be awful to be on your deathbed with a huge wedge of money in the bank? It's also true that by making a space we create a place for more to come in; this can be as true of a bank account as anything else.

Giving money away can have a very liberating effect. It's only in giving something that we truly understand what we have — generosity is a state of mind that can have far-reaching consequences for good. It also enables us to see the connection between the material world and the spiritual one.

I'm about to take a small risk of my own and tell you about something very profound that happened to me. It seemed like a nice way of ending this part of the book, as I started it, with a true story of my own, which had a large part to play in me writing this book in the first place.

Virginia Woolf • *Mo Mowlam* • *Einstein* • *Debussy* • *Mozart*

42

A Confession

To start with, I have to tell you that I'm not a Christian, and I'm not sure about the concept of a 'God' per se. Although I am not a Christian, I do believe that I have a strong understanding of the thing that people call the 'Christ Spirit'.

I went through what many people might perceive as a very strange period in my life, about 20 years ago. In fact, the whole thing was *so* intense that some of my friends thought I was going mad, or having a breakdown, or something. To me, it was more of a break*through*, not 'down'.

The events leading up to this very epic part of my life weren't great. I had split up from my partner after ten years. This was painful and protracted since we'd been together since our teens. I realise now that my partner was treating me with a huge degree of mental cruelty, but I can only see this from the position of hindsight. I thought, because he told me when he was going off with someone else for the weekend or whatever, that his honesty meant that he was essentially a good person. (In fact, this is also true; we were both very young, and had a deal of growing up to do and now, years later, we are very good friends). Anyway, this went on for years, and I was effectively

Capability Brown • *Frank Lloyd Wright* • *Norman Foster*

downtrodden to the point where I thought my heart was broken, and there was nothing I could do about it.

Then suddenly, I got very, very angry; I found the *real* version of the truth, and started to express how I was really feeling inside. While he was away with the latest flame, I bundled up all his clothes and things into black bin bags and left them outside the flat. I changed the locks and ripped the place apart to redecorate it, to get him out of there. This was about self-preservation. He'd never wanted to do anything interesting in the flat in case it affected the retail value. Well, now I didn't care about any of that! I needed to express myself, and my immediate surroundings became the object of that expression.

The more I worked out my own feelings, the more empowered I became. Sometimes, I felt as though I could rule the world, and I knew that I was a part of the universe, that all the distressing and disempowering things that had happened with my partner were a sort of bow, designed to pull me back so that once I could release myself from the confines of that bow, then, like an arrow, I'd fly really high!

The truth of the pent-up anger that I was finally able to release acted like a torrent in my life, and changed me in ways that there was no turning back from.

I started to feel things about people; I knew what was wrong with them physically, and knew that I could help them with the energies that were flowing through me. Were these angelic energies? Yes. I had no self-consciousness about going up to people and telling them where their pain was, and asking permission to take it away. I just let it all flow. At work, if people were arguing, I found that if I just let the energy flow through me, then they would gradually grind to a halt and the argument would stop; like a juggernaut going into reverse, the energy that was flowing through me would turn any arguments back the

Joan of Arc • Jimmy Page • Jimi Hendrix • Robert Plant

other way and the nasty, discordant atmosphere would be replaced with one of harmony and concord. But I could never call myself a 'healer'; none of this was my doing.

I felt so free, so alive; I would stop and talk to tramps in the street, sit with them, buy sandwiches and things for them. I slept rough for a while with a fabulous tramp lady called Rosie England, who was one of the wisest people I had even met. Like me, she had 'woken up' but found the everyday world hard to cope with in such a state. She had made a conscious decision to become a tramp, to help the many disturbed and often schizophrenic people that end up on the streets. I met one old Jamaican guy who stopped me in the street, crying; he told me that the energy of Christ was all around me, and asked me to look after his seven daughters who were all overseas. Another day, I was sitting in the sunshine outside a cafe with a friend when another old man came up, knelt at my feet, handed me a flower with shaking hands and, in front of my astonished friend, told me that I was Fatima. He was weeping in the gutter and I really didn't know what to do, so I just laughed, pulled him up and sent him on his way.

At this time I had an experience which showed me what had really happened when Christ had turned the water into wine in the miracle of the Wedding at Cana. When celestial energy flows through you, then it flows through everything you handle. I was pouring water from a jug for friends at a dinner when I suddenly realised was happening; it wasn't just water that they were receiving, but the Holy Spirit. The water was transformed by coming into contact with the Divine. I still feel silly calling it the 'Holy Spirit', because I'm not religious and it reminds me of all those tedious RE lessons at school – but it's the most obvious explanation and the most immediate description. It's the same energy that people call 'healing' energy, the same source that

Josh Homme • Kurt Cobain • David Bowie • Frank Sinatra

people call on to create music, or art, or anything at all that is done in a creative, ego-free way.

I couldn't stop this energy flowing; I didn't want to. I gave everything away (apart from the flat, half of which actually belonged to my ex). If it had been mine to give, I would have done so. Giving things away, freely, is a heady experience. Friends came round and took crockery, furniture, the TV, books, records; everything. I kept a telephone answering machine with a cassette that I used for music, some clothes, a toothbrush, but very little else. The pleasure in seeing all these things go was intense. The delivery driver who came to fetch my bed to take it to an orphanage turned out to be a spiritual medium. As we were moving the bed I heard laughter in the next room although there was no-one there. The medium heard it too; we stopped what we were doing and he told me that the laughter was from a sister that I had never known about, who had died before she was born, and who was now an angel. He took my hands and showed me how to touch her; I felt something invisible but hot, and something soft and very like feathers, and I cried and cried. Later I spoke to my mother about the loss that she had never mentioned to anyone, not even my father.

One day, I got on the bus with a bag of biscuits. As I stepped on, I could see everyone's souls shining out of their eyes. It was overwhelming, but also so beautiful, seeing this union, that the same spirit was shared by everyone. I went the length of the bus offering everyone a biscuit from the bag, knowing that the same energy that had flowed through me and into the water would happen with the biscuits. Everyone took them, was happy and smiling, except one person, who was afraid of me and looked away. Even the driver was happy. And I suddenly understood the meaning of the word 'communion'.

Bach • Carole King • W.M. Turner • Dali • Stubbs

All through this time, believe it or not, I was managing to hold down a very important and well-paid job; I was effectively my own boss although I did have employees to look after. I had freedom so long as I managed to get my work done.

A couple of days after the incident on the bus, someone came into my office and told me a story that a friend of a friend had told her. Someone had been on the number 18 bus a couple of days earlier when a woman had boarded, whom everyone had seen as an otherworldly being, an angel; she was apparently very bright and difficult to look at directly, haloed in blue light, and blessed everyone by offering them an ordinary biscuit from a bag. This vision had been shared by everyone on the bus.

How amazing, I thought, and then realised that this supposed angelic being must have been me. I'm not angelic. But the description was of me and my seemingly crazy actions on that day.

Since then, I learned to control the flow of this energy; I studied massage and healing techniques, and rarely talk about that intense time that lasted for about three months. I don't even think about it that often. I am no angel – that's one thing I know for sure! But the incident on the bus really made me think about the nature of the divine; perhaps we are all sparks of that divine light, waiting for a match of some kind to light the touch paper that will make that spark burn. I see that light in people, in trees, in animals, plants, in cloud formations. I am not a pagan, I am not a Christian, and I don't like definitions per se.

And I know now why some people call madness 'divine', and would never question any of those things that we read about, that happened in the Bible or elsewhere, as fanciful or invented. I experienced those same things. I know what the spirit of Christ is, because I have felt it and experienced it; but I am not a Christian. I didn't look for these experiences, and they didn't result in me becoming 'religious' or going to church, or

Bunuel • *Terry Gilliam* • *Degas* • *Diaghilev*

anything like that. I wrote everything down as it was unfolding, but I've never shared this before. Now feels like the right time to tell this story.

There's more, much more, and I know that there are many angelic encounters still to come. But this will do for now.

Leonardo Da Vinci • *Oscar Van Gelden* • *Chris Heywood* • *Galileo*